EVOLUTION

of

HUMAN
RESOURCES

The official list of contributing authors is as follows (alphabetical by last name):

Angela Bailey
Whitney Bishop
Teresa Cofield
Karen M. Dahlem
Michele Fantt Harris
Paula Harvey
Dawn O. Holzer
Eric Huber
Olivet Jones
Whitney Martin
Robert Price
Sandy Ringer
Linda S. Smith
Cassandra Tembo
Trasee Whitaker
Patricia Keene Williams
Lisa Withers

Book typeset by Kevin Williamson
Cover design by Kevin Williamson

Created in the United States of America

22 21 20 19 18 17 16   1 2 3 4 5

ISBN 978-0-9864371-8-2

Note from the Publishers

First, we want to acknowledge our authors and extend to them our sincere thanks. They have brought to us insights and expert knowledge from a diverse set of personalities and areas of professional specialty. We, as the curators, editors, and publishers, are the first to experience what they have been compelled to share here, and we relish the privilege of being first. Moreover, we've had the opportunity to *work* with each author, to bring our minds and attention together over something important, and the level of courtesy and professionalism we've come to expect from our authors is astoundingly high. We're grateful to them for setting and maintaining an impressive standard.

We would also like to thank our network of authors from Red Letter Publishing's Professional Series anthologies, including the authors of 2015's flagship *Rethinking Human Resources* and *Lessons in Leadership*. The authors of all our anthologies have shared with one another the special discourses of reading and writing, of professional learning, and of kinship, and it's a privilege to grow this community as the Professional Series continues into 2016 and beyond.

Human Resources is an essential arm of any company in the 21st century—but its place, purpose, and future have never been more uncertain. In this anthology, we consider what lies ahead in the evolution of Human Resources: how it will need to grow and change to succeed, but also, what we must do to drive that evolution. In the pages that follow you will find the next steps ahead for the uncertain world of tomorrow.

— *Cathy Fyock and Kevin Williamson*

A Brief Postscript—

If you would like to contribute to a professional anthology—We have another 2016 entry in the Professional Series, *Cultivating Culture*, which will open for reservations on July 31, 2016. Spots are filled on a first-come-first-served basis. *Cultivating Culture* is expected to release in November of 2016.

To ask any questions, propose topic suggestions, or inquire about custom projects, visit our website at RedLetterPublishing.com/Anthologies for FAQs and more information.

Contents

Angela Bailey

The Power of Partnership

Human Resources is a broad and complex profession, and it can be mysterious or even overwhelming for business owners and leaders. Much like law and accounting, human resources has many layers, levels, and divisions of expertise—and much like law and accounting, the regulations for human resources are always changing. No one person is an expert in every area and aspect of HR; add to that the possibility that a CFO, controller, or business owner is tasked with HR responsibilities, and suddenly it becomes easy to see how daunting HR can be.

For the HR professional and business leader, engaging a human resources outsourcing or consulting partner can remove a lot of that difficulty and contribute a number of benefits. This partner can work with you in numerous ways to support your objectives and move your business forward. If you can identify key projects or strategic objectives that require resources that you don't have, your partner can provide those resources and support so you can get the projects done. It's possible, too, that the "product" you need to present to, say, a Board of Directors will have more validity or influence if delivered by an outside consultant. Engaging an effective HR consultant to partner with you to accomplish those objectives and complete those projects can be a great move for your business. I feel a bit like a superstar when I think about the rewarding work I've been able to deliver and the people I've been able to help over the years as a human resources consultant and outsourcing partner.

Why Outsourcing?

Engaging a human resources outsourcing partner is a good business strategy for organizations of all sizes and industries. Ask yourself:

How can I make our business better?
How can I make our work team better?
How can I find the time and resources to get everything accomplished?
How can I keep the organization compliant?
How can I improve my performance and the performance of others?
How can I get some of this work off my plate so I can focus on other tasks or projects?
How can I structure our pay and benefits to attract and retain the right talent?
How can I recognize and reward our employees?
How can I . . .?

There are lots of questions and competing priorities for business leaders and HR professionals. Adding more (likely inexperienced) staff to those questions and problems is rarely effective. Engaging an HR outsourcing consultant to work with you as your partner can address your questions and provide solutions as well as resources for those competing priorities.

Engage an HR outsourcing partner to:
- Add HR expertise (they have access to certified HR professionals with a wealth of knowledge in different subjects)
- Target strategic initiatives
- Mitigate risk and stay compliant
- Promote positive engagement and resolve employee relations issues
- Collaborate for innovative solutions
- Streamline for efficient and effective operations
- Develop your leaders
- Spend wisely

There are countless reasons to engage an HR outsourcing partner, but the best reason is that it can move your business forward in ways you could never have moved it yourself. That's where the power of partnership begins.

Consider the small business without any internal human resources staff. For starters, engaging a partner with skills and expertise in human resources is less expensive than hiring an internal HR professional. Plus, if the partner is part of an HR outsourcing firm, then the small business has really engaged an entire *team* of HR expertise for less than the cost of one permanent employee. Human resources issues do not discriminate—no business is immune to issues concerning people, talent, retention, engagement, payroll, and the like. Plenty of HR laws apply to small businesses as well; many of the panicked or urgent calls received from clients and potential clients are the result of having a small business owner facing HR-related issues. Guessing your way through a harassment issue, for instance, or a wrongful termination complaint, is not the best strategy and often results in worse and more expensive outcomes.

For medium-to-large organizations with internal Human Resources staff, partnering with a human resources consultant provides opportunities and resources to address issues and move forward with key projects and strategic objectives. The HR outsourcing partner can provide neutrality for employee issues and investigations, or data and expertise for benefits design or wage studies. Perhaps the organization's HR leader needs to collaborate on revamping performance management, or restructuring the operations team. The HR partner can enhance the organization's existing HR staff by adding broad knowledge and experiences gained by working with a variety of organizations; as we know, it's healthy for organizations and work teams to add fresh and challenging ideas, which you should expect from your outsourcing partner. Then there is the issue of time; I'm not sure that I know any HR professional that *doesn't* have too much on their plate. The HR outsourcing partner can help with those finite resources of time and people.

Selecting the Right Partner

The key to experiencing the superstar feeling I described in the beginning is engaging the *right* HR consultant or consulting team as your partner. Selecting the right consultant depends on many factors. It's normal, especially for a business owner or finance professional, to be primarily focused on price or cost. Budgets and spending are important, but I'd be remiss not to say: if you're placing trust in a consultant to produce quality results, price should not be your determining factor. The cliché that "you get what you pay for" holds true, but more than that, you have to understand that identifying the right consultant and partner are based on criteria deeper than meeting your "ideal" price range.

Trust and relationship are key. In my experience, the most effective and exciting consulting partnerships are the ones where a high level of trust exists in the working relationship. Trust is feeling confident in the consultant or consulting team's competence, in their expertise, and in their ability to provide excellent and timely results. Trust is being able to reveal sensitive or even confidential information with someone who can help you. Trust is knowing that your outsourcing partner is invested in quality results and truly shares your enthusiasm and concerns. Trust isn't born right away and it may require the consultant to prove themselves in their behavior and by delivery on certain project milestones. I strongly encourage you to get referrals from colleagues when vetting HR consulting partners. Do your research, ask lots of questions, get referrals, and if you have the opportunity, catch the consultant in action (see them present or train at a conference, read their articles, and so on).

Establishing a strong working relationship is also key for a successful partnership. In the same way you'd conduct internal evaluations on your hires, evaluate how well you will work with the HR consultant or team. How well do you communicate with each other? Do they challenge you to think differently? Are you open to them challenging you to think differently? Will you look forward to working with them or dread their meetings and avoid their phone calls? Does their work style support your organization's culture and values? In other words: will you be fully engaged when working with them?

This should be true from the consultant's perspective as well. Not every organization is a good-fit client for that HR consultant or company.

Identifying why you need the HR consultant, and what you need from them, is also a critical piece of selecting the right partner. In my own time as an HR outsourcing consultant, I've experienced a version of "scope creep," when the project expands beyond its original scope. Scope creep isn't uncommon with outsourcing and consulting clients; they engage for a particular problem, objective, or project, then once the work begins they discover their needs are different or much broader in scope. Despite what many think, this change in scope sometimes means that they no longer have the right partner for the job. If the HR consultant has the expertise for the expanded scope, someone like me would gladly adjust our engagement and contract accordingly; however, the new costs might not be good for your budget planning. The point is this: give ample consideration to, and be deliberate about, your needs, and be sure to think critically about how an HR outsourcing partner can provide solutions to meet those needs. Every organization has a personality, a niche that they serve, and certain strengths and weaknesses. This is just as true for human resources consultants and outsourcing firms. Once you have a good grasp of your needs, part of your selection process should be identifying the HR partner with the expertise and strengths to meet those targeted needs. For example you may have an outstanding relationship with an organizational development consultant, but you probably would not engage them to complete a market wage study for your engineers. If your organization is in the hospitality industry, you may consider engaging a consultant that specializes in hospitality and is familiar with the dynamics and unique facets of that industry. You may have a variety of needs including leadership training, benefits design, recruiting and payroll. In that case you may search for a team or organization that can meet all of those needs, instead of engaging multiple consultants to cover the required expertise.

Making the Most of the Partnership

Now that you have identified the *right* HR outsourcing partner, making the most of that partnership largely depends upon your engagement with them. I've already suggested that you find an HR consultant that will challenge you to think differently. The power of partnership and collaboration is unleashed when you invite, and are open to, the consultant's challenges to your thoughts, ideas, perspectives, and even expectations. The consultant's role is to move you, your decisions, and your business in the right direction.

Let me explain something about challenging your expectations. By way of illustration: I have recently worked with clients from both large and small organizations to revamp their performance management systems. These clients entered our engagement expecting a performance tool that fit a traditional model of assigning ratings and focusing on past performance. They expected a revised, but still traditional, performance process. Working through the needs of the organization and identifying how to motivate best performance, none of these organizations ended up with a traditional performance model. Because these business and HR leaders were engaged in the partnership and collaboration, their expectations were allowed to be challenged which led to well-informed decisions on both sides—and ultimately better results.

Talk intentionally to your consultant and tell your story or stories. A good consultant will demonstrate active listening skills; they will listen to learn and understand your needs better. They will ask questions to understand your business, your industry and your culture, and most importantly, your pain points. A good outsourcing partner will expertly translate your gaps, needs, and pain points into solutions that work for you.

Share working expectations with your HR outsourcing partner. This goes beyond the engagement contract; discuss how you want the relationship to work. Are you inclined to be hands-on and involved in minute details, or do you prefer to provide direction and guidance and review milestones and results? Do you prefer email, phone, or face-to-face communication, and how often? Are there other people you want involved in decision-making or phases of the engagement? We have some clients that want to be contacted weekly, prefer on-site visits and the leader wants to be copied on every email to any of their employees; we also have clients that are only interested in the end product or results for each project. Our clients are across the spectrum with how they prefer to work within our partnership. Establishing that understanding from the beginning avoids confusion, irritation and disappointment. You may adjust these working expectations as trust is established and the partnership develops.

In many cases, client needs and their urgency will define the working expectations. Clients with urgent issues regarding an audit or employee complaints, for example, fall into a high-risk category. These engagements are not typically fun—we'd rather have our teeth pulled than suffer through most audits or deal with harassment investigations. However, strong and on-going partnerships often develop when the HR outsourcing partner helps the organization address critical issues like these and helps remove any high-risk threats. The HR outsourcing partner moves quickly and may engage other vendor partners depending on the risk issues. This requires an all-hands-on-deck approach, and unfortunately can be costly to the organization. The cost to remove the risk, however, proves to be much lower than incurring the high-risk consequences. Consider, for example, the risk of non-compliance with required 5500 filings, as we encountered with a few of our clients; the IRS charges a steep penalty per day, per benefit plan for missing or inaccurate 5500 filings. The cost to correctly file those 5500s (even if you engage the IRS delinquent filer program) is much lower than the penalties that can result otherwise.

Extreme or uncharacteristically high turnover is another critical issue that we are encountering more often. Low unemployment rates and the rapidly-growing Millennial workforce are contributing factors for turnover and the inability to recruit and fill positions; some say that Millennials will leave for 50 cents more per hour. We love working with clients on implementing recruiting and pay strategies to attract and retain the right talent. As we work with our clients on these issues, we sometimes discover that poor leadership, lack of communication, or just a bad supervisor are causing the high turnover. The business or HR leader is likely aware of the leadership or poor supervision problem; the HR outsourcing partner will work with that leader to better identify and solidify the contributing issues, and in many cases help the leader make the difficult decision to remove or change the leadership. Again, the goal all along is to partner with the client to provide solutions that will move the business forward.

Clients that are retained for several years experience a different sort of partnership success. These clients are not immune to urgent issues, but with strong engagement and partnership, they are less likely to fall into any high-risk categories. Annual training, benefits renewals, and improvement-oriented initiatives are typical needs for these clients.

Partnership Success

I love talking about successful outsourcing partnerships. As we've already discussed, engagement from the business or HR leader is as important as selecting the right HR outsourcing partner. I use the term *success* when an organization has truly moved from conversation about needs and issues to fully implemented solutions. In Human Resources—to mix metaphors for a moment—you're never across the finish line because your work is a moving target. Still, with successful outsourcing engagements, you've completed the first leg of a marathon.

I see outsourcing success occurring in four typical ways:
1. The organization has moved from high-risk to low-risk (e.g. compliance issues)
2. The organization has resolved critical issues (e.g. high turnover due to poor leadership)
3. The organization has effectively implemented a revamped process or program (e.g. recruiting and pay strategies)
4. The organization is performing well and is in improvement mode (e.g. as-needed recruitment, training, benefits renewals)

This is the power of partnership! An organization and their HR outsourcing partner spending time, effort and energy on improvement and future-forward initiatives, rather than spending the time muddling through old problems or dealing with avoidable risks and failures. Engage the right partner, be engaged in the partnership, and take advantage of the HR expertise and solutions provided by your outsourcing partner—so that you, too, can feel like a superstar.

ABOUT THE AUTHOR
Angela Bailey
SPHR, CCP, SHRM-SCP

Angela Bailey is the Manager of HR Outsourcing for HR Affiliates based in Louisville, KY. Serving the human resources profession for more than 20 years, Angie's experience has crossed many industries including manufacturing, higher education, consulting, non-profit, retail and healthcare. Her expertise includes benefits design and planning, compensation analysis, training and development and HR project management.

Angie focuses on results and takes pride in working with others to outline goals and identify strategies to achieve success. She is very passionate about her career in human resources and the opportunity to partner with business leaders and other HR professionals to develop policies, procedures, systems, and talent that will be the foundation of the organization's culture and success.

Recognized as one of the Top 20 HR People to Know in 2014 by *Business First*, Angie dedicates much of her non-work time to mentoring others both personally and professionally. Angie also presents and provides training on a variety of HR-related topics ranging from compliance to leadership, performance management, and wellness.

Angie also has a passion for worksite wellness, so she serves as the Wellness Co-Chair for KYSHRM and Wellness Chair for LSHRM, as well as on several local and state-based worksite wellness councils. She supports many non-profit organizations including Breath of Fresh Air (BOFA), American Cancer Society, and Shirley's Way (a local cancer patient support organization). Angie loves to sing, is a member of her church choir, and knows the lyrics to just about any eighties tune. With an adventurous spirit, you may find Angie enjoying cycling, hiking, rock-wall climbing, or just shooting hoops with her two young sons.

You may contact Angie at HR Affiliates using the email address angieb@hraffiliates.com or the office line (502) 485-9675. You can reach her directly at angelabaileyhr@gmail.com or at (502) 724-1177. Lastly, you can find her on LinkedIn and Twitter (*@angelabaileyhr*).

Whitney Bishop

The Way Forward:
Managing Personal and Professional Change

All's Fair in Mergers and Acquisitions?

When we found out what happened to our colleagues behind closed doors, the rumors started flying. They had 10 days to decide whether they would accept a transfer to Houston or take a small severance package and be let go. They had families. School was about to start. They all had histories with this small, family-run company. They never saw it coming. They were told not to say anything. They were told to get back to work.

A few years before, we heard the exciting announcement that the company had become so successful and grown so quickly that it had attracted the attention of a larger, better-established international company for possible acquisition. This larger company assured our existing leadership team that they would leave them alone to run things their way, allowing them to maintain the culture and the community ties that made them such a successful organization. At a certain point, things started to change, and those promises stopped being honored. What followed was a series of decisions, actions and an exodus—all which we should have seen coming, but never did.

Three Sides to the Story

From the top: there were metrics, margins and profits to consider, efficiencies to leverage, and systems to integrate.

From the middle: there was a growing sense of discomfort as they received directives from the top. They knew the culture was on the brink of change. They knew these directives and their consequences would start to change the relationships and the lives of the employees and their fellow leaders.

From the front lines: for the employees who felt more like friends and extended family, it was a slow-moving train wreck they mostly didn't see coming and had zero power to stop. The resulting silence, seclusion, and paralysis affected people at all levels of this situation.

What Happened Next

For the executives, the idea of putting these folks in a room and giving them a chance to express their frustration, their fears, and their concerns might have seemed like an unproductive use of time or, worse, a highly uncomfortable *and* unproductive experience.

But I knew that it was *precisely* the investment we needed to make in order to move forward. I finally got permission to hold this session, sans executives. As expected, many of the employees were distraught and disillusioned with everything that was happening; others with less at stake were more resigned to the changes and could admit they'd known this was always a possibility. There were people across the spectrum, but in 90 minutes, we were able to get clear about what everyone needed in order to move forward in this new reality.

Over the course of the next few months, the family-run company, the little company that could, was unrecognizable—many of the same faces, but virtually none of the spunk, the spark, and the joy that previously pervaded the space.

This is my own story, my own experience, but it's not a unique story. This is happening every day in the ever-changing worlds of business and industry.

The pace of change within organizations and in our personal lives has multiplied exponentially in the last decade, bringing with it waves of change and decision fatigue. No one is immune from them—not your customers or your employees, not your vendors and partners, not your stakeholders, not even your leaders.

Change is a stressor, and stress does have an impact on your overall well-being, including the likelihood of contracting an illness. (Consider Googling the Holmes-Rahe stress test and taking it for yourself to get an idea of where you stand.)

At any given moment in time, a significant percentage of your leaders, key supervisors, and employees could be in the midst of a highly charged and stressful situation. The timing of your organizational change initiatives need not be built around this; however, ignoring the fact that the people in your organization may sometimes be in a less-than-ideal state to make decisions or contribute will hamper your efforts and could have lasting negative effects.

Each of us has a unique relationship to change and resistance. When we honor it in each other, and ourselves, we are free to do our best work.

When someone's livelihood is threatened and their sense of security is shaken, how that person responds largely depends on these three factors:
1. Personal experience with change
2. Level of trust and relationship within the organization
3. Level of personal accountability and maturity

Suggestions for Moving Forward

Give space and time to allow people to discuss and share the impact that certain changes are having on them. If you think that *not* talking about it, that expecting them to roll with the changes and be quiet and do their work is a sound strategy—I can tell you, it's not. *Some* of them will roll with it; many of them will not. What will happen? They'll talk about it anyway—in pockets, online, while they spend their day looking for other jobs and complaining about their work environment. They will question their loyalty. They will begin to erode in front of you.

Support individuals by helping them learn how to better address and understand themselves during times of change. What are you doing internally to connect people to a better understanding of themselves during times of change? What are you doing to enhance their trust and relationships within the organization and encourage them? It's important, if you're going to make a real difference with people, that you empower them to ask for what they need in order to move forward.

Prepare your leaders to address the symptoms and challenges associated with big changes—extra time, extra one-on-one meetings, and whatever other steps may be appropriate and expected. Acknowledge the elephant in the room, in every room in the company; don't ignore it.

Encourage your leaders to *communicate, communicate, communicate.* Information and time are the number one and two things people need, respectively, during times of organizational change.

Leverage existing resources and add new ones. Connect employees to the resources available. Employee Assistance Programs, medical and life insurance, retirement planning, financial planning, personal concierge services—no matter what size organization you have, there are ways you can ease the impact of the personal and professional changes happening in the lives of those you lead and those you serve. When you do this, you help a person get to a place where they are capable of making better decisions and showing up in a productive and constructive way.

Ask the right questions, regularly. Create a culture that includes permission to ask for what you need, whether it's information, time, resources, or connections. Any of these elements have a tremendous impact on an individual's ability to make better decisions about how they'll move forward, or even IF they will choose to move forward.

Ask yourself and others these questions to find ways to move forward.
> *What assumptions are you making?*
> *What assumptions am I making?*
> *What would it look like if it worked?*
> *What do we have control over?*
> *What do we NOT have control over?*
> *What questions do you still have?*
> *What information do you need?*
> *When do you need it? How often?*
> *How do you need to receive it? In what form?*

The Way Forward

The modern workplace is a dynamic environment. External and internal factors are constantly shifting, requiring us to think differently about our options for growth and sustainability. Your people are in ever-evolving phases of change in their own personal lives. The confluence of these two truths necessitates a thoughtful and deliberate approach to moving forward.

When you ask the right questions of the right people at the right time, what unfolds is kind of magical. When you teach yourself to welcome change, embrace possibility, and leverage resistance, you move forward. When you connect your employees to the ability to do that for themselves, you create personal and professional growth that benefits the individual and the organization alike.

Whitney Bishop

Whitney Bishop is a change agent with a love/hate relationship with change. Her personal and professional experiences with change led her to a lifelong pursuit of learning how to navigate the ever-changing waters and become a guide for leaders who wish to do the same. In her consulting practice, Whitney serves leaders in the small business, non-profit, and corporate sectors.

Whitney is the creator of Make 3 Changes™, a breakthrough framework for moving forward during times of change. This practical and powerful framework creates clarity for those in the midst of a challenging situation and gives them permission to identify their desired outcome and commit to the changes they are willing to make to move forward. You can learn more about this tool by visiting www.whitneybishop.com.

She is a graduate of the University of Louisville's College of Education and Human Development with a Bachelor's Degree in Occupational Training and Development. A lifelong learner, Whitney is consistently engaged in learning and integrating new information and powerful experiences that will be of service in her own business and the leaders and organizations she serves. Her passion and privilege is creating personal and professional development experiences for leaders.

Whitney lives in Louisville, Kentucky with her husband, Lt. Colonel Chris Bishop, two great dogs, and one very fat cat. They are parents to Sarah and Parker, two creative, talented and resilient young adults, and doting grandparents to Acacia Cadence, Sarah's beautiful baby girl. They enjoy traveling and experiencing all that life has to offer, together.

Teresa Cofield

Change, Growth, and Culture:
How Companies Train New Hires for a Better Future

Take a look around. How many things that you see are the same as they were 5 or 10 years ago? At work, how many of the people around you were the same people around you when you started? People and organizations move, they grow, they change, and these changes are absolutely necessary. Businesses change systems and vendors. They adopt technologies to meet the needs of their customers and keep them competitive in a vigorous business climate. People chase dreams and new challenges and often find themselves seeking out new opportunities to expand their own knowledge and experiences. I think people and businesses both inherently understand that every change is an opportunity—an opportunity for progress, for growth, and to create bigger and better things for their futures.

According to the Bureau of Labor Statistics in 2014, the average time that a worker stays with the same company is 4.6 years. If we assume a person might spend 50 years working, that's almost eleven different jobs! With every new enrollment packet, a person will have to face the challenges of conforming to a new work environment and to new teammates who may or may not be well-suited for them. Owning a staffing company, and working in the staffing industry for many years, has given me the opportunity to see these challenges that people and organizations face. I've had the opportunity to experience the struggles from the standpoint of both the employees and the businesses and I've been able to see the patterns of conflict and conflict resolution that often arise.

One of my clients that experienced a great deal of workforce change was a company that started out with a small call center of about 10 people and quickly grew to over 150 people. Adding so many people to their call center, plus experiencing the turnover that call centers inevitably experience, created a volatile work environment. In addition to the changing faces of the call center employees, they experienced a great deal of change with regulations and services brought on by industry changes. Throughout the chaos, there were many things that this company and their leadership team learned (and did right) which helped shape their success and created an effective environment despite all the challenges they were facing.

There were three important initiatives that this company undertook in order to create the success they experienced in the call center. The first was implementing a thorough training program for new employees; the second was creating a structured set of expectations for call center employees; the third was maintaining a clearly expressed, positive company culture. Let's imagine that we are observing a group of new call center workers who were just hired by this company. On their first day, they come in and they're excited, but they're also very insecure about their surroundings. They are asking themselves "Are people going to like me?" or "Am I going to like this job?" Maybe they're even questioning their own ability to perform the work they're being hired to do. It's very normal to feel tentative when starting a new job, even when we've started new jobs a dozen times before. What the new employees need right now is predictability, and they need to feel like they are being brought into the team by competent leadership. The training program does this, and if the training is done correctly, it can set our new call center employees on a path to success.

The goals of any training program should *not* just be to train new employees on the function of the position, but also to set the tone for the new work group that forms as new employees enter the organization. So, as we watch our new call center employees get their training, we notice that they are highly dependent on the trainers and leadership for direction and to help create their vision for their future with the company. This dependency is driven by their fears and insecurities in the new company, and that's why it's so important that the new employees perceive their trainers to be competent and dependable. They need to be able to feel like they can be secure in their new position and group. They crave order and stability most of all, and creating a carefully-designed and structured training program will create stability for them so that they can move forward and start feeling inclusion and a sense of purpose within the company.

At this stage of the onboarding process, it's often easy to see which new employees will not take to the training or conform to company standards. Not properly addressing high-conflict or non-conforming members of the training group would be a disservice to the members of the group that would otherwise be valuable people in the call center.

The training is over and most of our new employees are still there, ready to get on the phones and start taking calls. Just like baby birds that start jumping out of the nest, the new employees are on their own and beginning to work independently, using their new skills developed from the training program. In a perfect world, everyone would follow their training and you would be able to predict how everyone performs in their roles, but as human resources professionals, we all know that it's absolutely *not* a perfect world, that each and every person has a different way that they like to do things, and now that our new employees are in flight they will want to add a little bit of their own flavor to their tasks. This is completely normal and sometimes acceptable, but having a structured set of expectations is so important in letting people know what is an acceptable variation and what is not an acceptable variation.

At this point, people are also looking around at others to develop their own personal work habits. For example, if they see people coming in late without consequence, they assume that is acceptable. They listen to the way other people talk to each other and the way they handle customers and they use that information to direct their own personal work behaviors. That is why it is so important to have structured expectations that are enforced, so that everyone is on the same page about what is allowed, about how they treat each other and how they handle customers. There is nothing worse than talking to a new employee about tardiness and having them point out how so-and-so is tardy all the time. You cannot expect punctuality without being fair and treating all employees the same across the board, regardless of tenure. Being treated fairly and equally is very important to an employees' sense of belonging to the group and essential in helping new employees develop loyalty to the company.

Now that our new people have been trained and have established themselves in their new positions, everyone can begin to feel the interconnection between the employees and there is a sense of predictability about the work environment. Our new call center workers are experiencing higher levels of commitment and stability, but the key to maintaining this cohesion is to create, and actively express, a positive company culture. When I think of great company cultures, I think of companies that are innovative and successful with both communication and teamwork. These companies attract the best of the best, and they can more easily keep the best of what they have. Spending the time and money to do fun and creative things for your employees is never a waste. A company culture is a way for a leadership team to express their core values and have other people within the organization understand the vision that they have for the company and for the people that work there. I think the saying is that *you become who you spend the most time around*. If that is true, then it's in the best interest of employees and their companies to surround themselves with like-minded people that share the same values, goals, ethics, and attitudes. The leadership team of the call center helped themselves by expressing their principles in a clear and concise way, which then created an environment for them to thrive through all of the change and carry on a fun, energetic, and creative company culture.

These processes in the call center example can be easily translated to many different groups and many different companies serving many different functions. The emotional bonding and group formation processes are much the same for a lot of companies, even on a smaller scale than in this example. The pattern is thus—first, the employee is hired and looks to leadership to help them develop purpose and company loyalty while conforming to company norms; second, the employee begins to express their own personal values and ideas in the organization and through the work that they perform; lastly, the new employee has a higher level of commitment and cohesiveness within the organization due to familiarity and comfortability with their surroundings. At all steps, the outcomes are highly influenced by the company culture and morale.

Change is inevitable for people and businesses that want to do more and want to be more. There is no progress without change, and understanding how to handle the natural change that comes with personnel fluctuations is essential in making the best of every opportunity.

Teresa Cofield

Teresa Cofield is a staffing and human resources professional with experience in flexible workforce strategies, team building, and human capital management.

Teresa started her career managing people in the United States Navy as a Cryptologic Technician Second Class where she served in both Operation Enduring Freedom and Operation Iraqi Freedom. She is currently a member of the Iraq and Afghanistan Veterans of America (IAVA) and actively advocates for veterans' rights and supports the needs of transitioning military members into private sector employment.

After her military duty, Teresa started a staffing company to service the recruiting and workforce management challenges of companies throughout the Triangle area. She owns and operates Skyline Personnel, a Raleigh-based staffing and recruitment firm that specializes in staffing for government and private sector companies. Skyline Personnel has experienced tremendous growth and success providing flexible workforce support and long term staffing solutions for companies, and they are proud to be one of the premier staffing agencies in Raleigh.

Karen M. Dahlem

The Importance of Collaborating with Employees During Times of Change

I believe it's important for leaders to collaborate with *all* employees during times of organizational change. It increases your effectiveness as a leader, creates trust, helps your employees feel valued, reduces resistance, creates buy-in, and positively impacts your bottom line. The various levels of management are normally included in conversations about organizational change, so this chapter focuses on lower-level employees who are many times forgotten.

Types of Organizational Change
Some examples of organizational change you may experience are:
- Leadership transition
- A rapidly growing or changing business
- Merger or acquisition
- Outsourcing
- New organizational initiatives

The Impact of Change on Employees
When an organization is going through change, employees are placed under new stresses and become less productive (see graph on the following page). Also, it is important to remember that employees going through multiple changes at one time (including personal changes) will be under even greater stress.

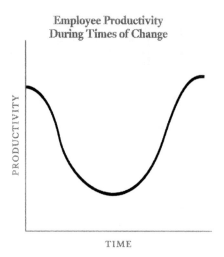

Well-managed change keeps decreased productivity to a minimum and shortens its duration.

Problems in the Lower Levels of Organizations

In *Seeing Systems*, Barry Oshry says the following about "Bottoms," the employees in the lower levels of an organization:

- Bottoms feel *oppressed* in the system.
- Others (higher-ups) make decisions that affect their lives in major and minor ways. Reorganizations happen *to* them; initiatives come and go; plants are closed; workforces are reduced.
- Bottoms feel unseen and uncared for. They see things that are wrong with their situation and with the organization that higher-ups ought to be fixing but aren't fixing.
- Bottoms feel isolated in the system. They don't have the big picture. There is no vision they can commit to and they don't see how their work fits into the whole.

During times of organizational change, input from lower levels of the organization is often missing, yet there is critical information available to leaders from this group of people—information that can help make the change a lasting success.

Who Can Help You Manage the Change Effectively?
So how can you manage change in your organization effectively and alleviate the Bottoms issues as described above? I recommend hiring an experienced external consultant who is knowledgeable about systems and change theory to work with you and your employees collaboratively. An external consultant is not a part of your organization's system and can, therefore, see the dynamics and issues in it more clearly than people who are part of the system. In addition, an external consultant is not constrained by the culture and may be able to speak more freely during various phases of the project, since the consultant is not an employee of those to whom he or she reports during the project. Also, employees often speak more openly with an outside person who is not a part of the organization's system.

What if your organization is hierarchical and not used to collaborating with employees during times of change? A consultant will help you work within the cultural parameters of your organization and will also suggest new ways to work within your organization to optimize effectiveness.

Effective Change Management
The chart on the next page, from *Organization Development and Change* by Cummings and Worley, is one of my favorite models for managing change.

MOTIVATING CHANGE
— Understanding Need for Change —
— Creating Readiness for Change —
— Overcoming Resistance to Change —

CREATING A VISION
— Energizing Commitment —
— Describing a Desired Future State —

DEVELOPING POLITICAL SUPPORT
— Assessing Change Agent Power —
— Identifying Key Stakeholders —
— Influencing Stakeholders —

EFFECTIVE CHANGE MANAGEMENT

MANAGING THE TRANSITION
— Activity Planning —
— Commitment Planning —
—Management Structures —

SUSTAINING MOMENTUM
— Providing Resources for Change —
— Support System for Change Agents —
— Developing New Competencies and Skills —
— Reinforcing New Behaviors —

A consultant can work with you to manage each phase of the model to the left.

There are several points during the above change process where input and interaction with employees at lower levels is important, "Motivating Change" being the most critical. During this phase, it is important to create change readiness and to work to overcome any resistance to change.

Employees generally need to be given a compelling reason to support change. They need to understand the pressures the organization is facing and why change is necessary. Often there must be pain in the system in order to create motivation for change.

Employees also need to understand the new vision, what exactly will take place during the change, and other pertinent information about the change, which lets them know specifically what is changing and the impact it will have on their lives. Giving this information reduces rumors that create confusion and anxiety and decrease performance.

One of the most effective ways to overcome employee resistance is to collaborate with them and gather data from them. The data collected is extremely helpful as you plan and implement the change. It will also surface problems and barriers to implementing the change successfully.

The Collaborative Process

During this collaborative process, the consultant gathers the data from employees in person, by phone, or via computer survey. The questions are created jointly by the leader and consultant and are based on the specific change the leaders are planning, as well as any known issues to date. Even the simplest questions can surface key information about resistance to change and issues that may impede a successful implementation.

Next, the consultant analyzes the data and finds the themes within it.

The themes are reported back to the leadership and those who completed the survey at a feedback meeting. At this meeting, the consultant facilitates a discussion around the themes, then the group determines problems, gaps and opportunities, prioritizes them, and creates a list of recommendations for leadership to take forward as they plan and implement the change. This information can then be incorporated into the "Activity Planning" portion of the "Managing the Transition" phase.

The feedback meeting is also an opportunity to discuss the organization's new vision, from the "Creating a Vision" phase. During this time, employees learn more about how their work fits into the new vision, why the changes are necessary, and how the changes will impact their lives. It's an opportunity for a robust discussion.

Sometimes, if the organization is large, there will need to be a series of feedback meetings. In this case, a combined list of recommendations is given to the leadership team to use as they plan and implement activities during the change. Often, a core group of employees is assigned to work on a task force that helps plan and implement the change.

As a result of this collaborative process, employee questions, ideas and needs will be heard and taken into consideration during the planning and implementation of change. They will be involved in decisions that affect their lives, will feel that leaders have seen and cared for them, and will have the big picture, as Barry Oshry recommends in *Seeing Systems*.

This process also creates a real commitment to the change, since employees will have been involved in creating it. Employees begin buying into the change in advance, which keeps decreased productivity to a minimum, and shortens its duration.

Stories of Change

I have seen the successful engagement of lower-level employees during times of change. I have also seen a lack of engagement from these employees and the problems that ensued. The following examples are simple, yet illustrate the issues discussed in this chapter.

Many years ago I worked with a new leader of a division of a corporation. He was interested in gathering data from employees as he began his tenure. We asked a few simple questions in the interviews, and the data that came from it was very helpful for that new leader. The data was positive and included information on employee concerns, what they needed, and how to engage them. But when I discussed the themes of the data with him, he changed his mind; he decided not to finish the collaborative process. Over the next few years, this leader had issues engaging and motivating his people. He focused solely on numbers and people in upper management, disregarding the data we gathered. The result was apathy in the organization and, in turn, decreased productivity from the people he was leading.

I recently worked with a large association in the midst of rebranding and changing their name. They knew of some resistance to the change and wanted to be sure they were making the right decision. We created a process in which we surveyed every level of the organization and all association members. The data showed us where there were pockets of concern and resistance to the change. We disseminated the results of the survey to all who participated, and then conducted several feedback meetings. In the end, the resistance dissipated. I find that using this process—caring and listening to people's ideas and concerns—often decreases the resistance to change dramatically. This particular change was very successful. Leadership used the questions and issues from the survey data as they created their communications strategy for the transition. The survey data was useful in many ways as they transitioned to the new name and brand.

Summary

During times of organizational change, it is important to collaborate with all levels of the organization. The lower levels of the organization are frequently omitted from the planning phases of change. If you include all levels in the planning, you will gather valuable data that will help you create buy-in, reduce resistance, create trust, and increase your organization's effectiveness.

ABOUT THE AUTHOR

Karen M. Dahlem

MSOD

The first thing to know about Karen is that she is passionate and committed to the work she does. She believes that change is inevitable, and she thrives on helping others see change as an opportunity for growth and success.

Karen is President of Dahlem Consulting, a business that partners with organizations to manage organizational change. She also works with individuals to manage personal change.

She has a Master of Science in Organization Development (M.S.O.D.) from American University in Washington, DC. She is fluent in French, Spanish, and English and has significant international experience. She has lived and worked in Western and Eastern Europe, South America, North America (including Canada and Mexico), Asia, and North Africa.

When the project calls for a larger team, she collaborates with a consortium of Organization Development consultants whose expertise is also available to her clients.

Karen worked for over ten years with Computer Sciences Corporation and their clients (such as TSA, Ascension Health, General Dynamics, Nissan, Bombardier, Aon, and United Technologies) on large-scale IT outsourcing projects. She managed organizational change and communications and also lead various other teams.

Karen has also consulted with many other organizations, both corporate and not-for-profit, in a variety of industries.

Clients trust Karen because of her dedication, honesty, tenacity, leadership, insight, diligence, open communication and facilitation skills. Karen builds relationships that work, and many of her clients call her again when new challenges arise.

For more information or to contact Karen, please visit her website at www.dahlemconsulting.com. You can also reach her by phone at 502.836.7403 or by email at karen@dahlemconsulting.com.

Michele Fantt Harris

Develop Bench Strength through Succession Planning

"Hi Michele. I just wanted to let you know that the regulators will be coming to NCB in three months and they want to see our written succession plan. Now is the time for you to write about our learning and development strategy and tie it to the succession and replacement plan that the executive council has discussed. Please prepare the plan and let me see it in a few weeks."

Oh, *great!* I thought. Now where do I begin?

In this chapter, I will outline what I did to create a succession plan that would be acceptable to our board, auditors, and compliance and regulatory agencies. I will identify the thought patterns that HR must consider, as well as the succession plan management and leadership development strategies that all lead to the final plan.

What is succession planning and management? SHRM defines succession planning as "the future-focused practice of identifying the knowledge, skills, and abilities to perform certain functions and then developing a plan to prepare multiple individuals to potentially perform those functions . . . it is a focus program of keeping talent in the pipeline and is generally at least a 12-month process of *preparation and not pre-selection.*" Succession planning is not replacement planning where you focus on identifying replacement for key personnel with little or no development of those potential successors.

To begin the Bank's succession management process, I needed to address a few questions to define the scope of the succession plan:
- Does the Bank want to focus the succession plan on executive positions or delve into the middle management level as well?
- Is the company considering dual career paths for different positions? Can credit personnel move into the lending area or vice versa?

- Does the Bank build its bench strength from within or does it go outside to get the talent?
- In what types of activities is the company willing to invest to develop potential successors?
- What kinds of internal and external resources does the Bank have to support career development?
- Is the Bank willing to invest the funds and time to develop an internal successor for a future position(s)?
- Do we have qualified people ready to fill key positions now and grow the Bank in the next 3 to 5 years?

Luckily, I knew the answers to these questions, as I'd had previous conversations with members of the executive council about talent management challenges. The Bank has established leadership development programs such as LEAD and Managing at NCB. We hire external coaches to work with management to address their leadership challenges, and we hold management lunch-and-learn programs to address specific management issues. The Bank invests in building bench strength in technical areas by sending top talent to the Stonier Graduate School of Banking and the Graduate School of Banking at the University of Wisconsin. We've taken the time to develop and train high-potential employees in the technical and management issues of NCB.

Next, I reviewed NCB's strategic plan to identify current and future priorities. How will the Bank reach its goals and objectives that support the mission, vision, and core values? What are the retirement and attrition projections for our staff? What is the turnover rate for the past five years, and why are employees leaving? Will new technology affect the delivery of the Bank's services and change staffing patterns?

Succession planning can go in two main directions: choosing by position or choosing by person. The Bank's succession plan does both. The succession plan focuses first on positions at the executive and managerial level, then reviews the incumbents in key bank roles. When using the organizational focus by positions, I had to consider what positions would be key to implementing future strategic goals of the bank. Were there specific executive or management positions that were unique to NCB? Were there particular positions of influence within the banking industry, the cooperative market, or required regulatory or compliance positions? What were the jobs that had long learning curves? Which jobs required extensive experiential learning?

After identifying the specific executive and managerial positions to include in the succession plan, I identified the current and future staffing levels for those positions. What competencies, knowledge, skills, and abilities were needed to carry out the functions of those jobs? Does the bank have qualified staff that has the requisite competencies and experiences to lead the organization forward?

To develop the strategic workforce plan, I met with each member of the executive council to discuss succession planning for their department. I reviewed the organizational chart of their department and identified the key roles and functions for future success of each department's leadership. We identified the current incumbents in those roles and discussed their readiness for promotion, their challenging areas, and their future training and development areas. Here are some of the questions that I asked at the succession planning meeting with the executives:

1. If you should leave the Bank suddenly, who would you recommend to replace you? Are there talented high-potential employees internally ready to fill your shoes? Would we need to recruit externally?
2. What are the key roles in your department? Do the current incumbents in those roles perform at a commendable level? Is your department at risk for losing any high-potential employees?
3. Do you have adequate bench strength to fill the key roles in your department? Where are there skill gaps?
4. Can we formalize education, training, mentoring, and coaching activities to enhance the technical and/or leadership skills of these high-potential employees?
5. What department positions will become obsolete or eliminated? What new skills and knowledge will need to be developed to meet the future strategic needs of the Bank?
6. Have you prepared development plans to maximize the potential of the incumbents in the key departmental roles? If not, what would they look like?
7. If there are no potential successors in your department to fill given key roles, what external sources would you identify to recruit a potential successor for your position or other key roles in the department?

A high-potential employee at the Bank has the ability to move into one or more key roles at NCB. High-potential employees have requisite technical and leadership skills and model the core values of teamwork, integrity, customer focus, diligence, flexibility, and innovation.

The evaluation of high-potential employees is a subjective process based on the opinions of the executive council members who supervise them. Therefore, it's very important that the succession planning discussion meetings be honest, trustworthy, and transparent for the success of this initiative.

After gathering employee data from each of the executives, I was then ready to write the succession plan identifying who the potential successors were for all members of the executive council (EC), as well as key managerial roles who report to each EC member. I included development plans for all persons identified in the succession plan, along with the timeframe that the employee would be ready for their next promotion or temporary role assignment. The development plan for each identified employee would include specific projects and assignments to help them develop multiple competencies, keep them engaged, and build the Bank's talent pipeline.

For your quick reference, below is the table of contents for the Bank's succession plan:

Table of Contents
Overview
Identification of Key Executive and Management Positions
Defining Core Leadership Competencies
Overall Succession Planning Executive Summary
Succession Plan Summary
The President
The President's Succession
Conclusion
Appendix (may include replacement charts or succession planning grid)

As another reference and inside look, here is sample succession plan documentation for an (imaginary) Chief Administrative Officer position that could exist at NCB:

> After assessment of potential candidates and discussion with the current Chief Administrative Officer, it was determined that Jane Smith will be developed as a succession candidate for John Doe if he were to leave his role as Chief Administrative Officer. Jane will require two to four years of operational management experience in the areas of Human Resources and Facilities Management to be ready for this role. Jane is the Vice President, Human Resources at the Bank and is a graduate of the HR School of the Graduate School of Banking (GSB). It is recommended that Jane attend

the executive leadership program at the Graduate School of Banking. To engage her in the daily facilities and operation functions of the Bank, Jane will be groomed by John to be the liaison to the internal and board operations committees. She will assume the liaison role within one year while John remains on the committee to mentor her.

Since John will be retiring in two years, Jane has time to develop one of her direct reports to replace her as Vice President, Human Resources. At this time, the two HR managers are likely successors to Jane, but neither has expressed interest in the role. Jane will determine the career aspirations of both managers; if either manager is interested in the Vice President role, s/he must obtain human resource management certification and agree to serve as project coordinator for a major HR initiative, such as the HRIS implementation or performance appraisal management. The interested manager must attend the HR School of the Graduate School of Banking. Jane will continue to mentor and coach both potential successors.

The third step in succession planning management is to implement and communicate the succession plan. It is critical that you share information about the plan during *and* after the implementation of the plan. Getting top support from the CEO and the board establishes succession planning as a priority, and other executives will help keep the succession planning initiative successful.

The final step in the succession plan management is to continually evaluate and revise the plan. Determine if the succession plan is meeting timely objectives and goals identified in the plan. Report progress to your organization's executive team and board of directors on a regular basis. Succession planning is a continual process; you will need to evaluate the effectiveness of the succession plan and make revisions as needed. Constantly updating our succession plan will ensure the Bank is ready for the changing workplace and increased regulatory and compliance needs of the future.

In closing, here are some helpful tips about succession planning and management:
1. Start the career development discussion with employees during the hiring process. In addition to the position they are applying for, discuss the types of advanced roles they could potentially qualify for now or develop in the future. Gauge the employee's interest in building a career with the organization and advancing their leadership skills.
2. Communicate openly about the organization's succession planning and management process. Let employees know that the organization is willing to prepare them for roles with increasing responsibility. Do not guarantee a promotion or a

new opportunity, but express to employees that they can grow and develop with the organization.

3. Although Human Resources is responsible for developing the succession plan and monitoring the process, succession planning is a responsibility that is shared by everyone in the organization. HR should involve board members, the senior leadership team, managers, and employees at all levels of the organization. Everyone has responsibility to develop and coach talent to meet the future needs of the organization.

4. If you do not have the support of the C-suite, build a business case for succession planning and align the plan with future business objectives. Succession planning and management have many benefits for an organization, including identifying skill gaps and training needs among talent, retaining institutional knowledge, boosting morale and retention of long term employees, adapting to changing demographics, and addressing talent shortages in certain areas. Explain that succession planning can mitigate the effects of an unanticipated vacancy in a key position.

5. Technology can simplify succession planning and management. Learning Management Systems can enhance your succession plan by tracking employee performance, identifying skill gaps, and noting employee qualifications and education.

6. Use a variety of adult learning methodologies in your succession planning and management including mentoring, coaching, job shadowing, leadership training, and cross-training. Job development is not limited to promotional opportunities. Consider job enrichment or job enlargement as means to enhance an employee's skills and competencies.

At National Cooperative Bank, we believe in developing our employees. Several of our senior leaders started in the Bank's Professional Development Program (PDP) and now lead major strategic components of the Bank. Although we lost a few of our top talent along the way, we always keep them as valued customers and supporters of the Bank. We even have a "Boomerang Club," employees who left the Bank and returned to the same role or a management position later!

Michele Fantt Harris

SHRM-SCP, SPHR, GPHR

Michele Fantt Harris is the Executive Vice President, Human Resources for the National Cooperative Bank, NA in Washington, DC. A certified Senior Professional in Human Resources, Michele holds the SHRM-SCP and SPHR certifications and the Global Professional in Human Resources (GPHR) designation.

A seasoned HR professional, Michele has worked in human resources in education, non-profit, healthcare, and the insurance industries. Her books, *What's Next in Human Resources* (Greyden Press, 2015) and *Rethinking Human Resources* (Red Letter Publishing, 2015) are groundbreaking publications for human resources professionals and entrepreneurs.

Active in many human resources organizations, she is a past president of the Human Resources Association of the National Capital Area and the former Black Human Resources Network. A member of the Society for Human Resource Management since 1985, she served on the Society for Human Resource Management national board from 1996 through 2001 and is a past chair of the SHRM Foundation Board of Directors.

Michele completed the Results Systems Coaching program and is an Associate Certified Coach (ACC) through the International Coach Federation and a Certified Career Management Coach (CCMC) through The Academies, Inc. She served on the board of the Delta Research and Educational Foundation from 2008 to 2015 and is currently on the board of the Children's STEM Academies.

She received her Bachelor of Arts degree from the University of Maryland, a Master of Administrative Science from Johns Hopkins University, and her Juris Doctorate from the University Of Baltimore School of Law. Michele teaches the SHRM Learning System at Prince George's Community College and Catholic University.

Michele is a native of Baltimore, Maryland, and currently resides with her husband in the District of Columbia. Michele can be reached at michele.harris19@gmail.com.

Paula Harvey

Going Global 3.0:
It Is Not What You Expected!

Leading HR in a global setting is quite complicated and can be unexpectedly frustrating sometimes. It requires collaborating with others in ways that you can't imagine prior to this kind of work. This chapter will discuss a real-life case study of the author's experiences and lessons learned. In this chapter I will discuss some information to give you a better understanding of what it truly means to *go global*; I will relay some challenges and lessons learned in performing global HR work; lastly, I will emphasize what it takes to be successful in global HR.

Three years ago, I spoke at various conferences about the challenges of Going Global in HR. Now, after living the global HR life, I have several real-life experiences and learning moments to share. One of the key things I have learned is that you must be able to laugh at yourself and find the positive in anything. Before taking a full-time global HR role, I had only dabbled in global HR as a speaker and consultant. Being immersed is a totally different experience—and a lot less glamorous than I expected.

In the eighties, I had the opportunity to be an exchange student twice, in high school and then in college. This influenced me to major in International Business. I envisioned having an exciting business career jet-setting from one place to another. Reality set in, upon graduation from UT Austin, that at my young age I was not going to get that international job, as I was told I had to pay my dues. So, I went into HR with the aspiration of someday performing HR on a global scale.

After a successful 25+ year career in HR and running a successful consulting business, I decided to finally change my path, sell my business, and go after the global HR position. In preparation I had obtained my GPHR and then become an instructor for the exam preparation. So I felt like I knew my stuff thoroughly, at least from a textbook standpoint.

In January 2015, I took a position as head of HR for the US and Canada division of a construction products manufacturing firm. This firm is owned by a huge consortium based in Mexico City and owned by some of the richest men in the world. I was so excited and had my rose-colored glasses on, ready to collect passport stamps.

In the first two weeks, I realized quickly that I was in a very different situation than I had ever been. I was on the executive level of my US subsidiary, but had a strong dotted line to the Mexican HQ. I felt that I had many bosses and at times they were not in agreement on the course of action. I also had major cultural understandings or misunderstandings to deal with on an everyday basis. I felt that I had been dropped into a global whirlwind at 100 miles per hour.

Companies have many ways of going global in current times. A company can just dabble in it and send some folks overseas, potentially importing or exporting goods and services and little else—on one side of the spectrum. On the other hand, a company can easily be "born global" due to the Internet and social media. It is a very strategic choice for a company, to decide what shade of "globalness" they ought to engage in. In my experience, many companies aspire to be truly global, but few *are* truly global. Due to control issues, ethnocentric beliefs, and fear of risk and exposure, most companies are only moderately global when they tout they are a global company. Usually the parent company will call the shots and see the world through their home-country lens.

Some other important factors that will influence HR's role are the size of the company, whether it is a public or private company, and the HR education level of the HR staff. You may be a decision maker in the US division, but have little influence on the larger global company. In smaller companies, you may be able to make quicker decisions, but that may also involve being more transactional since there are fewer HR staff members. In large organizations you may be able to specialize more, but most likely you will have less strategic influence in the company (depending upon your position).

Private companies are sometimes able to accomplish initiatives, including HR initiatives, faster since they may have less red tape. Public firms are required to show shareholder value, and it may take more effort, including making the business case for HR initiatives, to get those HR programs approved and executed. It also is highly dependent on the management style of the leaders, to whom hopefully HR is a valued member of the executive group.

I have discovered that many HR employees across borders were homegrown and rarely formally educated in HR knowledge. So many HR types have learned their jobs through the school of hard knocks and on-the-job. If you are formally educated or HR-certified, you may face reverse snobbery or even jealousy in some places. It is not a compliment to be told that you are "too smart for this job in this company."

During my career of studying global business practices, I now have discovered that performing HR duties in a global setting is very different in reality. One thing has rung very true for me: the key to success is to have a global mindset. This is not a skillset learned overnight, but instead over years of experience and exposure to doing business on a global scale. In a definition from SHRM, a *global mindset* is an ability to take an international, multidimensional perspective that is inclusive of other cultures, perspectives, and views.

Working in a global organization, it is very important to have an open mind and to be able to see many shades of gray even when you feel, personally, that an issue is black and white. You must remember that you work in Human Resources, and the "human" part is both variable and very important. You must be able to be tolerant of others who are not like you, to be empathetic of others' feelings, and to remain open to new ways of thinking about HR-related challenges.

Another key to success in a global environment is to be able to live and breathe the "S" word: *strategic.* Many HR professionals complain that we have overused the word *strategic* and it has just become a business buzzword. But it should be practiced, and in my daily HR rituals, I am constantly thinking in my head, "How does this decision or action or idea affect the *strategy* of the company?" For companies who use the balanced scorecard, this is should be very intuitive, as this is the premise of that system. For others, it is a business imperative to have strategic thinkers in leadership. When you are working in a global setting, decisions that are made can have the ripple effect and touch employees on the other side of the globe. HR must participate in creating their organization's global strategy.

Several years ago I created a top 10 list to enable HR professionals to keep their seat at the table. The notion of "getting one's seat at the table" has been bandied about for a couple of decades in HR circles. But I truly believe it is not about "getting," it is about "taking" one's seat and keeping it by earning the right to stay in the C-suite. On the following page is my list with a newly-added global flourish:

Paula's Top 10 List

1. Be the Consummate Global HR Professional
   a. Know Your Stuff including the latest and greatest in the countries where your organization does business.
   b. Learn some words of a foreign language and the cultures where your organization is based.

2. Obtain and Maintain Deep Expertise in at least two functional areas of HR
   a. One area must be talent management for the global HR professional.
   b. The second area depends on the needs or industry of your organization.

3. Use Smart Business management global skills
   a. Study how business is conducted across borders and how to use the "S" word.

4. Understand different points of view (P.O.V.)
   a. Have several viewing points for each situation.
   b. Be willing to think outside of the box.
   c. Be an advocate for diversity and inclusion, key global themes.

5. Hire "A" talent everywhere, as it will make you an HR Hero
   a. Surround yourself with smart people.
   b. Learn how to negotiate and understand compensation systems.

6. Make the tough decisions sooner rather than later
   a. My mantra is Hire Slow, Fire Fast—take the time to find the right employee "fit," but if Dr. Jekyll becomes Mr. Hyde, rip off the Band-Aid.

7. Execute[3]
   a. Understand the needs of your global company and execute them well.

8. Keep searching for tables, hallways, and water coolers
   a. Join in and meet with employees in all locations. It is better to put a face to an email or phone voice.
   b. HR cannot live alone on a desolate corporate island. Global HR professionals must be a strategic partner to all stakeholders.

9. Ethics and Integrity
   a. Global HR professionals can really struggle with ethics since it does not have the same meaning all over the world.
   b. Remember to always do the right thing when no one is looking. You have to be able to live with yourself.

10. It is all about the team, each and every member
    a. No Lone Rangers.
    b. HR should not live on a deserted island.

Finally, it is most important to be passionate about your job. It does not matter where you are from; humans from all cultures recognize someone who is genuine and loves what they are doing. Passionate positivity will run off on others and get more work accomplished. It also makes the day go by very quickly. As a bonus, add some smiles to your interactions with people, because it is good relationships that make the world go 'round.

Paula H. Harvey

MBA, SHRM-SCP, SPHR, GPHR

Paula H. Harvey is the VP of Human Resources for Schulte Business Systems in Hockley, TX. She has worked in the retail, services, construction and manufacturing industries. Mrs. Harvey has 29 years' experience as a Human Resources generalist.

Paula earned her Bachelors of Business Administration in International Marketing and Operations Management from the University of Texas at Austin. She has also earned her MBA with a concentration in Human Resources Management from the University of North Carolina at Charlotte.

Paula is a Senior Global Certified Professional of Human Resources through SHRM and HRCI. She completed, at the top of her class, the OSHA 501 train-the-trainer course and is an authorized OSHA trainer. She has achieved the Manager of Environmental Safety and Health Programs (MESH) certification and the Advanced Safety Certification (ASC) from the National Safety Council.

Using her HR certifications and MBA, Paula teaches several business-related topics, especially in Human Resources. She is also an internationally-recognized speaker on global and strategic business issues. She has published articles on HR topics and co-authored two books with other HR professionals.

Paula is an active member of the Society for Human Resources Management (SHRM) having served as the SE Membership Advisory Council (MAC) Representative, NCSHRM State Director/President, and President of Union County HR Association and Charlotte Area SHRM. Paula is currently a member of HR Houston on the University Liaison committee. In 2005, she was awarded the NCSHRM "HR Professional of the Year," and in 2014, she was recognized as the NCSHRM HR Humanitarian of the Year for her efforts in mentoring HR students.

Dawn O. Holzer and Linda S. Smith

Learning That Lingers:
Designing Training for Skill Transfer

When my fourth-grade class was studying the solar system, I couldn't understand how a heavenly body could both *rotate* and *orbit* at the same time. I was studying at home and getting increasingly frustrated when suddenly my dad starting moving the living room furniture against the walls. He put me in the middle of the room; I was the sun. Then he started walking around me in a big oval, explaining that he was the earth and was orbiting me. Once I understood that, then he started to spin in slow circles—while still making his orbit—to illustrate rotation. *Eureka!* I still remember the feeling of deeply understanding, finally, what the words *rotate* and *orbit* meant together.

This chapter is about learning—or, more specifically, about *designing learning that works*. Generations of corporate trainers have designed and delivered learning according to the best practices of another time, largely based on theories from educational research on how children learn and process information. It's time to move the furniture against the walls and try something different. In this chapter, we'll combine our insights from 40+ years of combined practice, along with current research into how the brain works, to share techniques for designing learning that lingers and makes an impact in the workplace.

Let's start by clarifying terms. Just what do we mean by learning that "lingers"? Baldwin and Ford have defined transfer as *the degree to which trainees effectively apply the knowledge, skills, and attitudes gained in a training context to the job.* Transfer is the holy grail of training, the thing we're all seeking. Many corporate trainers work hard to develop great platform skills. They're funny, engaging, prepared, knowledgeable. Their content is spot-on and their materials are beautiful. None of that is worthwhile, however, unless training participants are able to take what is learned in class and *transfer it* back to their jobs. Learning for its own sake is valuable in an undergraduate literature class, but not when an employer is expecting bottom-line results.

Three key factors influence training transfer. Certainly the **learners** themselves have some bearing on how well they learn a skill and whether they implement it on the job. In addition, the **workplace environment** matters. Are managers and co-workers willing to support new learners? Does the corporate culture support trying new things? For the purposes of this chapter, however, we will focus on a third component of transfer, the one that is most solidly within the control of the trainer: the **design process**.

Within the design process, let's consider the elements of **Planning, Execution, and Reinforcement**.

Planning

If we want learning to linger, we have to start planning for it long before participants arrive in the classroom. This can be accomplished by talking to stakeholders, as well as interviewing and observing learners doing their jobs. We'll need to identify the gaps in what is currently happening and what needs to happen; that is, are there new tasks or processes we need to teach? External consultants must also work to understand the corporate culture and norms since these will impact the participants' ability to transfer learning.

A solid starting place for design is to discover what learners need to *know* and *do* in their jobs. For example, when training leaders on how to manage performance, it is important that they *know* organizational policy as well as applicable laws. However, they also need to be able to *do* effective reviews and conduct themselves well as leaders; so, the training will need to include knowledge, but focus on building skills that can be applied to the job.

This is also the time to consider job aids, follow-up materials, action plans, on-the-job application, accountability conversations, and so forth. We'll share some specific techniques when we talk about reinforcement, but know that the time to *plan* for these activities is now.

Execution

A primary consideration in the Execution phase is narrowing the focus of training. Too often, organizations try to get the most out of a session by asking for too many diverse topics, by shortening the time allotted, and by including as many participants as possible. Trainers—both internal and external—are sometimes so accommodating that we don't push back to establish a reasonable scope that allows for real transfer. While content *may* be king, we assert that less is more; it's better to ensure that whatever you train will persist and transfer to the workplace.

If transfer is the goal, we have to ensure participants aren't overloaded with content and that we are providing ample time for skill practice. In our research and experience, we've learned an effective formula for transfer is to spend one-third of the allotted time teaching the content participants need to *know* and two-thirds of the time on reflection and application of what they need to *do*. Yet how often have we gotten so engaged in explaining an interesting theory that we've cut short our time for robust practice? It's important to discipline ourselves to spend time on the right things.

With both organizations and individuals increasingly pressed for time to devote to professional development, technology offers us another option. The popular trend of the "flipped classroom" facilitates a focus on practice time; this technique allows for delivering core concepts online, or even through pre-work, and then using the classroom time to embed concepts, correct misunderstandings, address questions, and engage in valuable skill practice.

Not all skill practice is created equally; the more practice simulates real world conditions, the more likely it is that transfer will occur. Flight simulation, for example, attempts to replicate the conditions pilots will face so they gain skills in a safe environment. By contrast, most leadership and interpersonal training requires teaching general principles that can be applied to unique situations; an example would be teaching the principles of negotiation and allowing opportunities for practice, realizing that no scripted scenario can anticipate all conditions. Effective practice opportunities cannot be treated as an after-thought, but should be intentionally and thoughtfully designed with plenty of time allotted. We recommend spending twice as much time debriefing exercises as conducting them. Participants will learn through practice; they will extend that learning through sharing insights, hearing the perspectives of their peers, and connecting to workplace challenges.

Scientists have learned much in recent years about how the human brain works; it's time for learning professionals to incorporate some of this knowledge into our training design. Let's think back to the story we shared at the beginning of this chapter. From many years of schooling, why did that particular lesson about the solar system stick so powerfully? What is it that causes some memories to be so strongly embedded we can recall them in great detail, whereas we sometimes have trouble remembering things that happened yesterday? We may remember smells, tastes, and even sensations decades later when other stimuli fade. Just what is it that makes something memorable— and how can we capitalize on this in training design so *training* is similarly memorable? After all, participants are unable to transfer learning if they don't remember it!

Research outlines a few types of long-term memories which are relevant to learning. These include **Episodic, Semantic**, and **Procedural**. By using these to inform our training design, we can help solidify experiences so they have staying power.

Episodic memory is the easiest to retrieve and is associated with events; it includes location, time, and emotion. Tap into this by taking learners outside the classroom for hands-on experiences or by using the physical space in the room to embed concepts. For example, when teaching concepts that fall along a continuum, we will ask participants to "line up" according to where they fall on the continuum. Or we may post ideas around the room and ask them to "vote with their feet" by physically moving to where the ideas are posted and staying there to discuss concepts with their colleagues. This use of the space, tied to the learning, sticks with participants, as evidenced by the fact that hours or days later, participants will still refer to where they were standing when a concept was discussed.

Semantic memory is memory attached to language. Interestingly, it is the most difficult to retrieve, so if we're just talking and participants aren't *doing*, they are less likely to remember and transfer. Think of the stereotypical college lecture hall and reflect on how much you remember from Philosophy 101, and you'll understand what we mean!

Procedural memory relies on repetition to be embedded in our subconscious; this includes what is commonly known as "muscle memory." For example, when teaching front-line job skills in an environment such as manufacturing or food processing, repetitive practice with feedback is beneficial. When nursing students are learning to give injections, they (thankfully!) practice on oranges before practicing on actual patients. Eventually, these skills become automatic, so that the person performs the task correctly without consciously thinking about it. When developing automatic recall, there is no substitute for repetition. Many of us grew up using flashcards for this purpose, but now, of course, there's an app for that! Electronic versions of this technique (Quizlet and many others) make it easy to create tools for repetition of key concepts.

Even for non-technical skills, repetition is a useful technique. When a learning professional teaches a model, then has participants discuss it in small groups, then facilitates an application exercise, this repetition of the concept allows it to become ingrained in learners' procedural memories.

It's worth noting, on the subject of lingering learning, that emotional experiences both good and bad are responsible for some of our strongest memories. In fact, the more emotionally charged an event, the more vividly it is remembered. We're not suggesting you deliberately bring learners to tears, but there *is* some value in carefully facilitating experiences that bring up strong emotions and even push people outside their comfort zones. This can be done through ropes courses, activities that may create frustration or put people into conflict, or exercises with tight timelines that simulate a sense of urgency. For example, when facilitating change management programs, we typically use an exercise that brings out the frustrations that people feel during times of shifting expectations. We can think of numerous times when a participant has walked out, given up, or gotten angry. When carefully debriefed, these emotional reactions created powerful learning not just for one individual but for everyone involved.

These insights into memory explain the impact of experiential learning. Well-designed activities and simulations create lasting impressions because they tap into different memory receptors; they may be episodic, semantic, and emotional all at once.

Beyond utilizing the power of memories, there is a final classroom factor that can influence transfer. Does it matter who delivers training? Absolutely. Research suggests that *the trainer* may also influence how much information is retained by participants and transferred to the work environment. Effective trainers set the tone for how learning will unfold. They know when to push a group out of a comfort zone and when to encourage, when to have the group actively moving and when quiet reflection is more appropriate. The right trainer can teach content, employ strategies to aid retention, and perhaps even increase participants' motivation to apply new learning. Thus, we recommend carefully matching the trainer to the audience and culture. Subject matter experts, tapped to train in many organizations, can become effective trainers with adequate mentoring and development.

Reinforcement

We've discussed two important elements of designing for transfer: planning and execution. The final element, reinforcement, concerns what trainers and participants do after a session has ended.

If we expect learning to linger, we need to create opportunities for participants to plan how they will apply new skills on the job, what obstacles they will face, and what resources might be helpful. Action planning is a technique practiced by many trainers, but too often it is a rushed exercise in the last moments of a class—or worse, a vague suggestion to participants as they gather their belongings to leave. This is unfortunate. According to research conducted by Hutchins, having learners set specific goals for how they will use new skills in their jobs is *the most consistent predictor* of transfer. Consider using contracts between learners and an accountability partner—a coach, manager, or peer—to increase the likelihood they will follow through on their commitments. In our ongoing work with one large organization, there is a clear expectation that participants meet with their managers after the initial class in a multi-part series. During this meeting, they establish expectations, set goals, and plan for how they will follow up with one another throughout the program. Thanks to this simple approach, managers are more involved; they actively encourage skill practice and consistently give feedback related to goals. Training participants are held accountable by partners inside and outside the classroom, creating greater transfer of learning.

Another aspect of whether learning lingers is related to the timing of the training's delivery. Early in our careers, the norm was for clients to schedule multiple consecutive days of training. In recent years, we have seen more organizations favoring a series of shorter sessions, extending a learning program across months rather than days. While the reasons often have to do with time pressures of the work, an additional benefit is a structure which allows for better retention and transfer. Do you remember cramming for exams? Sadly, so do we. People can only absorb so much new information before our brains are "overloaded." It's much more effective for participants to absorb small chunks of learning, go back to work and apply what they've learned, then come back for more. When delivering full-day or multi-day sessions, it's vital to build in plenty of application, feedback, and reflection to embed concepts and skills.

A final element of reinforcement comes in the form of follow-up from training sessions. Earlier we discussed the value of skill practice. Of course, practice is not limited to training time. Learning can be extended before and after a program—before, to enhance readiness to learn as in the flipped classroom model, and after, to allow opportunities for further practice. In addition to structuring practice, it can be useful to send periodic reminders of important information. Not surprisingly, there are a number of tools and technologies that can set these up for you, and even organizations that will handle all the reinforcement messages on your behalf. However, trainers can also push out reminders and assignments for free using email or the organization's intranet. Reinforcement needn't be high-tech to be effective.

Final Thoughts

Our opening story would be perfect if Linda had grown up to become an astronaut! While it didn't quite turn out like that, important learning nonetheless lingered from that experience—the recognition that when one teaching methodology doesn't work, another one is in order. When efforts to convey knowledge aren't getting the intended results, it's up to trainers and designers to start moving furniture and doing something different in their planning, execution, and follow-up. To reflect on the words of Sir Winston Churchill: "It is always more easy to discover and proclaim general principles than to apply them." As learning professionals, our mission is not to do what is easy— proclaiming general principles—but to do what is best for learners and organizations. What is best is to design and deliver learning that lingers.

Dawn O. Holzer

BCC, SPHR, SHRM-SCP

A Board-Certified Coach and talent development professional, Dawn draws from 25+ years of business acumen in leadership and organizational development. She partners with a diverse mix of national and global organizations in a variety of industries to drive talent development initiatives that result in sustainable individual and organizational shifts.

Dawn began her career focused on shifting organizational culture, improving quality, and developing leaders in a multi-hospital healthcare system. Next she joined a division of American International Group where she headed up high-potential development and succession planning. In 2005, Dawn opened her own consultancy, Pathway Leadership Consulting.

As president of Pathway Leadership Consulting (see www.PathwayLeadership.com), Dawn works with a variety of organizations and their employees around the world. A gifted facilitator, Dawn is able to quickly understand her clients' culture and challenges, integrating this knowledge into her programs and coaching. She is also a master trainer for Discovery Learning International and often partners with other consulting groups to implement large-scale initiatives.

In 2011, Dawn partnered with Linda Smith to create CaseCards, a company which provides resources geared to learning professionals, with the goal of helping them make a lasting impact (www.CaseCardSolutions.com).

Dawn holds a B.A. in communication as well as an MBA, and she is qualified to administer and debrief a multitude of assessment tools and simulations. She routinely shares her leadership and talent development expertise by speaking at regional and international conferences.

Dawn lives with her husband in Mt. Pleasant, South Carolina, where she enjoys running, time on the beach, and hanging out with friends.

Linda S. Smith
M.Ed, SPHR

Since beginning her corporate training career in 1992, Linda has been privileged to work with diverse organizations across industries, ranging from internationally known firms to small family businesses. With her broad experience as a learning professional, Linda has a deep understanding of how people learn and is able to apply this knowledge in fresh and practical ways. Her candor, diplomacy, humor, and energy make her a valuable coach, trainer, speaker, and consultant.

Linda is the principal consultant at Splash Performance, where she focuses on designing custom training solutions which enable individuals and organizations to maximize their potential. Linda is passionate about facilitating self-discovery through coaching and training. She is a talented facilitator who challenges participants to explore concepts in unique ways—always with the goal of immediate application. Learn more about Splash Performance at their website, www.SplashPerformance.com.

Linda's credentials include a B.A. from Wake Forest University and a M.Ed. in Training and Development from NC State University. She maintains the Senior Professional in Human Resources designation and is qualified to administer a number of organizational development tools and instruments. She is a well-received speaker on topics related to workplace learning at both regional and international conferences.

Linda and her co-author Dawn Holzer created CaseCards, a company which provides resources geared to learning professionals, with the goal of helping them make a lasting impact (www.CaseCardSolutions.com).

Linda lives in Winston-Salem, North Carolina with her college sweetheart, three delightful children, and one unruly dog.

Eric Huber

Curtain Up!
Theater-Based Learning in the Workplace

As a self-proclaimed "theater geek," I have never repeated the adage "everything I need to know about life I learned in kindergarten" when speaking of myself. Indeed not. Everything I need to know about life, for me, was learned through theater. To be honest, I don't really remember much about kindergarten, except the small carpet samples we used to take our naps on and the sugar cookies with the horrid red jelly centers we ate at snack time. Perhaps as foreshadowing to my priorities later in life, what I do remember fondly from kindergarten and beyond are the annual holiday shows produced by the music teacher and the art department, and the many plays or artistic presentations allowing us to share our newfound knowledge with the school and our parents in creative and artistic ways.

This passion for theater and arts would continue throughout my life as a hobby, not a profession. Theater was something I enjoyed, but not without learning many lessons. It taught me about commitment, community, collaboration, teamwork, fellowship, and meaning—all elements of a successful and engaged workforce. Theater and the arts influenced my core values and helped develop leadership and management philosophies throughout my career. For me, it has universal application: most of us have been in, or seen, some form of theatrical production in our lifetimes.

While theater isn't my profession, elements of theater began to play a large role in my professional career as a practitioner of Organizational Development. In fact, the theater has a similar profession called *dramaturgy*. Dramaturgy is the study of dramatic composition and the representation of the main elements of drama on the stage. It can also be defined, more broadly, as shaping a story into a form that can be acted out. Dramaturgy gives the work or performance its structure; it's also a tool to scrutinize narrative strategies, cross-cultural signs and references, historic sources, genre, and ideological approach. It is practice-based as well as a practice-led discipline. Sound familiar? Does the word *consultant* come to mind?

To understand the application of theater in the workplace, it's important to briefly review its roots. While the history of theater can be traced over the past 2,500 years, most are familiar with some aspect of the Western tradition of Greek theater, mostly developed in Athens. It was part of a broader culture that included festivals, religious rituals, politics, law, athletics, music, weddings, and funerals. Participation in the many festivals, as well as attendance as an audience member, was an important part of citizenship. Civic participation also involved the evaluation of the rhetoric of orators in performances in the law-court or political assembly. Both the court and the assembly were understood as parallels to the theater and increasingly came to absorb its dramatic vocabulary. To aid in the correlation of theater to the modern workplace, consider citizenship as "culture" and assembly as the "organization."

The concept of theater-based learning is not necessarily new, but it is not commonly practiced. Theater was simply something I incorporated casually until I read an article originally published on SHRM.org in April 2010 reporting on the efforts of Dr. Mark Rittenberg. In the 1970s and 1980s, Dr. Rittenburg used theater-based exercises to build cultural bridges and develop mutual respect between Israeli and Palestinian students. His work thereafter focused on the power of communication, assessing organizational culture, and developing strategies for organizational root-cause analyses. I wasn't alone in my focus, and Dr. Rittenberg's efforts became a catalyst for me to learn a more formal approach to theater-based learning in the workplace.

As Human Resource professionals, the opportunity to practice theater-based skillsets presents itself beginning with the hiring process when we put out an ad (a "casting call") for a position (a "role"). When interviewing for a job, are you not essentially auditioning for a role, a specific part in a production called "work"? Your talent is generally assessed by a series of questions in the beginning. If the person asking questions remains interested, you may also be asked to provide examples or demonstrations of your talent. These generally take the form of typing tests, personality assessments, samples of specific desired skills, and behavioral interviewing techniques.

In essence, the director or manager is looking for someone who brings something special to the role, something unique that makes them stand above the crowd. Ancillary items such as how well they work with the remaining talent or cast (team), or how many in the job market have the same skill sets, may also be assessed. How we package our skill sets, or how they manifest themselves through our behaviors, may be what determines the successful candidate. The mantra, "Hire for fit, train for skill" values individuality over a person's skill set, especially if the role is customer-focused. Skills can be taught and behaviors can be modified, but personalities are forever.

Each of us possesses the capacity to assume multiple roles in a day. Often, we are called upon to be mother, father, husband, wife, boss, friend, and so on. Historically, we've referred to these roles as "different hats." Putting on a hat sounds easy, but actually assuming a role requires much more.

After "auditioning" for a former position, I accepted the role of Director of Organizational Development with a large multi-specialty healthcare organization. As is typical, I was required to attend New Employee Orientation. At this organization, New Employee Orientation consisted of a handful of presenters all with allotted periods to introduce specific aspects of the organization. The full-day event was sponsored by the HR department, yet there was no facilitator and no apparent coordination. Presenters had no idea what others were speaking to, so often material was duplicated or, worse yet, contradicted. New employees spent the day being flooded with information and yet no inspiration. Needless to say, the curtain needed to go down on that production, and fast.

A full year later, approaching the day as a theater-based event, we crafted an experience that not only informed our employees, but inspired them. It focused on culture — not so much on what we do, but how we do it. Our orientation became more about establishing "citizenship" within the "cast" of healthcare. We created an environment (set) with memorable visuals. We approached the content of the day like a story with a defined beginning, middle (intermission), and end. We outlined what was expected of a person in the role of an employee within the organization. We even coached our presenters to be engaging with their content and ensured they knew what other speakers were discussing so the various presentations ("acts") could flow seamlessly together.

And there were understudies! Recognizing that orientation was critical to building the desired culture of the organization, two facilitators were at the ready should one of the regular cast members (speakers) not be able to make it. In fact, one of the cultural philosophies we adopted earlier in the process, "Life's a Stage — You Are Always On" was explored as part of the curriculum.

New Employee Orientation should be seen as an opportunity to inspire staff to make a difference, regardless of the industry. Presenters should know the "plot" of what others are discussing. Equally important is recognizing that, just as no theatrical production is perfect, neither is any organization. We are, and always will be, works in progress. A critical question we should always ask ourselves as leaders is: "Are we living up to the promises we've made?" If not, this is a real-time opportunity to make an adjustment. You have to know your audience.

Although not someone known for his theatrics, Galileo once said, "All truths are easy to understand once they are discovered: the point is to discover them." Orientation should be about discovery and it's our role to provide our employees with a theater and experience that maximizes the potential for real discovery to happen. Begin by being authentic, and build skills for your staff to discover authenticity.

In our industry, healthcare: knowing that employee and physician engagement directly correlate to the quality of patient experience, we shifted our focus from the employee to the physician. Historically, patient care has been measured primarily by clinical quality. While clinical quality remains critical to patient care, the "experience" of the patient is now taken into consideration and measured as well. By incorporating theater-based learning skills into our Clinician Observation/Coaching Program, a communication-focused learning event, we were able to provide our clinicians with feedback and concrete examples of what a visit should and could be with minor adjustments.

Consider, for example, a scenario in which a doctor is running late for an appointment. Most physicians would consider an apology for running late to be sufficient. A more theatrical approach might look like this: the doctor knocks on the door and pauses a brief moment before entering. Doctor enters the room and says, "Mrs. Smith, thank you for waiting for me. I apologize for running behind schedule." This is a perfect example of how a minor change in the script and blocking can *dramatically* affect the tone of the visit (the "production"). The patient (audience) is more engaged and more likely to accept the apology. If the doctor had said, "I am sorry for running late" without acknowledging that the patient waited, the tone of the visit would be very different; the doctor would clearly have put himself before the patient.

At one extreme, some doctors may say, "What if I don't mean it when I do that?" In a situation like this, it's best to say nothing rather than say anything you didn't truly mean. At risk is coming across as insincere, sarcastic, or fake. Theater-based learning would suggest exploring the doctor's feelings or motivation a bit further to discover a place of truth through exploratory questioning.

Theater-based learning is an argument against "faking it until you make it." It goes deeper. You don't have to be a theater major or professional actor to incorporate the elements of theater in your organization; you simply need the desire to create a meaningful culture based on truth. Our role is to discover that truth, and to put it on its stage where we can share it for everyone to see.

Eric Huber

Eric has over 20 years of professional experience in talent development, organizational development, Leadership, and Physician Recruitment combined in both the private and public sectors.

He has dedicated the last 10 years to a large multi-specialty healthcare organization creating a comprehensive service initiative from the ground up, focused on patient care, employee engagement and physician engagement. Eric is a certified faculty member of the Institute for Healthcare Communication teaching Clinicians Communication–based curriculum and as a Clinician Coach. To support this endeavor, Eric co-created a comprehensive physician observation program to enhance and sustain learned skills. Due to the success of the program, Eric was asked to present key elements at the Press Ganey National Client Conference in Orlando, Florida.

Eric has also presented to customer service-focused programs throughout Springfield, Illinois, as well as the Physician Wellness Conference for the Sangamon County Medical Society.

Eric holds a Bachelor of Arts in Business Administration as well as a Masters in Communication from the University of Illinois in Springfield, Illinois.

Eric is an active member of the Society for Human Resource Management, a Professional Member of the National Speakers Association, and a Fellow of the Association of Staff Physician Recruiters (FASPR). Eric also holds multiple certificates from the Association for Talent Development (ATD) including Leadership Development, Coaching, Facilitating Change, and Immigration. He is also certified in Everything DiSC, Drake P3, and Real Colors Training.

Eric is owner and founder of Complex Whine, LLP (www.complexwhine.com), whose mission is to discover the richness, depth, intensity, meaning, and authenticity of interpersonal communication and bring balance and harmony back to our lives.

Olivet Jones

The Cavalry is Not Coming:
The Corporate Woman's Field Guide to Respect, Recognition, and Reward

The cavalry is not coming. It's a poignant realization every woman in leadership—or who aspires to be —will encounter at least once on her journey to the top. My moment of truth came as I sat in a cushy office on a high floor of a downtown corporate headquarters in Chicago. My contact there, also a woman, had just dropped the news (and not too gently) that I would not be paid what others—read *men*—in my field are paid. *Why not?* Because a male senior executive up the food chain fundamentally believed that "we don't *have* to pay women that much." As I sat there absorbing this rather surreal moment, I realized that I was completely on my own. What could I have done to prevent this? Who was at fault? And most importantly, what could I learn from the experience to ensure that it never, ever happened again?

Forget that we had pulled together a five-country team to conduct research on, of all things, women's leadership. Forget that our work was recognized as top-drawer. Forget that six months of hard work was already complete, wrapped, and in the can—or that we had a contract. In short, forget that we had saved a whole lot of people's bacon. As the hard truth of it set in, fiery tears of anger began to well up. The "70 cents on the dollar" slogan took on a whole new meaning. I wish that I could tell you this was around the year 1965. It wasn't.

Rolling the timeline forward—as I sat down to write this chapter, I frankly struggled with how to get my arms around such a big topic in a relatively small space. What could I say that might bring a fresh perspective on the inequities women in business often face? Some great, well-researched articles have been written about the importance of sponsorship and mentorship for women. And there has been much discussion in print about how women can gain and leverage power, visibility, access, and opportunity. Indeed, the conversation about what it takes for women to advance is not a new one by any means.

With all this solid research and good advice available, something monumental ought to be changing—right? If we women have been empowered to succeed, why are the numbers of women in higher levels of leadership moving incrementally rather than exponentially? Where is our voice in places of power, influence, strategy? Why are turnover rates among women in management so often disproportionately high? And, if we don't do a better job of getting it right, what will be the impact on businesses as a new generation of women move into the workplace and opt out earlier than most corporations would like?

Here's one observation: we *have* done a good job of empowering women to succeed, however they define success. So I wonder: have we been equally effective in *equipping* those women, the ones who can (and wish to) take on greater responsibility in the corporations that employ them?

My choice of the word *equipped* is deliberate. If I begin with the premise of the Coaches Training Institute—that people are naturally creative, resourceful, and whole—then I conclude that we women don't need fixing. And in that spirit, I won't offer the up the "10 things every woman must do" to maximize her potential in the corporate arena.

Rather, I propose that it may be time for a shift to a different kind of dialogue within ourselves, our spheres of influence, and even our communities. The dialogue I envision doesn't lend itself so much to scorecards, checklists, and ticket-punching. This fresh approach to dialogue demands a different depth of individual and collective reflection that supports the collective ability to deliver on business results.

To contribute to that dialogue through this article, I've put on my coaching, consultant, strategist, and listening hats and revisited hours of conversations with men and women around this topic over the last few years. I do not offer this as a one-and-done solution; rather, think of it as the beginning of our field guide, ruminations from the trenches and from a place of curiosity and discovery. You are sincerely invited to add your own wisdom and insight and understanding as we shape the framework for a shared credo.

The remainder of this article looks at some of things we have learned along the way from two perspectives. One perspective is what we women might reflect upon as we shape our own career trajectory. The other is the role that Human Resources can play in moving the ball forward.

It starts with a vision. One of my mentors taught me that "if you don't know where you're going, all roads lead to anywhere." As I coach women (and men), I am continuously surprised at how many of my clients, from the emerging-leader level to the C-Suite or equivalent, cannot really articulate a personal/professional vision. They can talk about business objectives, job titles, and levels of responsibility—but no clear vision. (*Vision*, as we define it, is what you are seeing on the horizon of your life.)

I love to ask this question: "In a world of infinite possibilities, what would your life be?" Common responses range from blank stares to momentary flare-ups of real passion, which often are followed by a shrug of resolution that conveys the thought *it'll probably never be*. Too often, I see women confuse a vision with a job title: *I want to be vice president. I want to get to the stock option level.* Good goals, perhaps, but not a vision.

As HR professionals, we can help women to think beyond the title to the "something that" vision of their lives and work that speaks to impact, contribution, legacy. In one scenario, a high-potential coaching client threatened to literally throw me out of her office. As we engaged around her vision, she brusquely and repeatedly threw up reasons (only some of them sound) that her dream job could never be realized. . After a full 30 minutes of this, she abruptly excused herself from our session. As she rounded out of the room, I heard her say sharply, "They've sent me an idiot for a coach!"

Fortunately for her, today she's living her impossibility. And it only took her 12 months to get there. What was the differentiator? The dogged ability to keep asking a simple question: "If the impossible were possible, what would have to be in place for it to be possible?" Shifting her perspective from "why it can't be" to "what would it take for it to be" was the key.

If you can accomplish your dream by yourself, you're not dreaming big enough. I can't take credit for saying that. I first heard it from multiple entrepreneur, author, and pastor TD Jakes. In one of his presentations, he talked about the importance of your team—not your "downline reporting group," your *team*. As a coach, I help my women clients identify at least six categories for their team: experts (technical or role-specific), business literacy mentors, powerful influencers, master corporate navigators, truth-tellers, and cheerleaders. Each plays a different role. Your groupings may be different, but I believe these are the fundamentals.

In our HR role, we provide a great benefit when we can help people draw on our knowledge of our organization. We can direct our stakeholders to engage with others whom we know might serve their needs. We may even provide access to people they don't know whenever appropriate. Because HR cuts across so many dimensions of the organization, our unique perspective can be of great value to supporting women in their development as leaders.

Find your table pounders—and cultivate lots of them. I shudder when my coaching clients tell me "my boss is very supportive of me." As gently as possible, I ask a simple question: *and who else?*

Folk at even the higher levels of employment can miss this point. It's unlikely that the support of your boss is enough to get you to your highest level of aspiration.

Any HR professional who's ever sat in a succession planning or 9-box session will tell you that one voice never carries the day on anyone's behalf. (Well, *maybe* if that voice is the chairman and sole stockholder). It is critical for women to develop a cadre of "table pounders"—people who will go through walls, burn political capital, and generally not rest until somebody provides a really, *really* good reason that you're not growing or advancing or whatever. Most essentially, you need people who have the power to speak on your behalf and cause other people to listen.

Become sponsor-ready. Sylvia Hewitt and others have written extensively on the importance of sponsorship for women. The truth is that it's important for everyone. The difference is that men often *think* they didn't have a sponsor (or want you to think they didn't have one). In fact, anybody who has ever achieved the highest level in corporations has had a sponsor whether they knew it or not. It was only when women and people of color fully entered the mix that language began to emerge, and programs evolve, that were intended to create the opportunity for structured, overt sponsorship. Unlike mentoring, sponsorship is based on a sense of knowing you, a sense of comfort with you, and the belief that you are trustworthy. The truism is that a mentor talks to you, a sponsor talks *about* you.

What makes you sponsor-ready? Good sponsorship begins with building rapport and evolves to a relationship of ease and trust. For the individual, the first step is doing your due diligence to discover what's important to the individual you wish to sponsor you. I shared this approach with one client who felt it was too invasive and potentially manipulative. After some discussion, she saw that businesses spend considerable resources understanding customers and clients and devising ways to best connect with them. Is cultivating a sponsor any different?

Once a woman has identified potential sponsors and developed an initial connection strategy there are three questions that I strongly encourage her to consider:

1. How do I want to show up?
2. What do I want a potential sponsor to know about who I am that is *not* on my résumé, and why?
3. What's my ask, exit, and follow-up strategy?

Another aspect of sponsor-readiness preparation for women is being literate about your business. I am often asked whether it is "appropriate" to contact certain people in pursuit of career advancement. Of course one must use some common sense—don't call up the CEO to say hi. Still, I agree with a comment from a CEO client, who told me, "I will find time for anybody in my company who is interested in my business and making it better." I know him well, and he's serious about honoring that commitment.

As HR professionals, we have a wonderful opportunity to support business literacy. If women are to be viewed as trusted business advisors and real players, we need to know more than just our own jobs. What keeps our leaders up at night? How does the business make its money? What drives profit? What are our key metrics? Where does our role fit into the big picture? HR professionals can create opportunities big and small to support women in this arena.

Break the feedback code. I heard a great quote once: "Your enemies have information about you that your friends won't tell you." A little Machiavellian perhaps—but useful. The point is that you have a brand out there in corporate land, whether you have crafted it and cultivated it or whether it has just sprung up from seed.

This lesson was brought home to me by a dear colleague who taught me that feedback is a gift. One day she called to tell me that, to my surprise, nobody on a particular high-visibility team liked me! One of the blessings of my character is that I'm pretty much made out of Kevlar, so I did what all good coaches and consultants do when we don't know what to do, and I asked her to tell me more. My friend explained that in this group's culture, people approached meetings a certain way: you travel in time to gather at the hotel by 5, you have about 45 minutes of chit-chat, you go to dinner as a group for an hour or two, and then you tuck away in your hotel room by 8 to prepare for the next day. Except that nobody told me that—so, as I hopscotched across the country, I set my travel so I'd be on the ground by 8 and in the hotel by 10 each evening. My objective was maximizing the work day while blissfully ignoring the value of building relationships.

Hopefully you will see that not knowing this group's norms, I just did what worked for me. To the group members, my actions translated as "cold, distant, and disinterested"— not a good brand for a transformation agent. Because we are friends, my colleague gave it to me straight; then she helped me design a simple strategy that didn't require much more than a change of flight schedules. But what if she had never told me?

As HR professionals, we know a lot about what's being said about whom, by whom. Professional ethics and integrity dictate that we maintain the privacy of those conversations, lest we invite a lawsuit. Still, we must ask ourselves where we *can* intervene. This may require a thoughtful, restrained approach, but it can be done, as my mentor did for me.

Take somebody with you. Talent, talent, talent: the great differentiator in today's business environment. We gather, analyze, and study mega-gigabytes of data in search of predictive patterns of behavior that drive engagement and talent retention. And, given the shift of generational perspectives, this data is vital to winning the talent wars. Expanding the capacity of the business through expanding the bandwidth of people, is mission-critical for the contemporary woman leader. Soft skills are not so easily dismissed; emotionally intelligent leadership can be one's new value proposition.

Taking somebody with you is not limited to developing lower level of talents. For the woman of power it can also mean providing thought leadership to the men who work alongside them as colleagues and superiors. I would note that I am not recommending that men avoid "doing their own work" in gaining awareness of matters pertaining to gender in the workplace. Still, a well-placed question or insight can go a long way in shifting the conversation in purposeful and productive ways.

For HR professionals preferring this kind of thought leadership can be tricky. One client, a Corporate Vice President of Diversity for a 24,000-person enterprise, shared this insight: "HR is rewarded as a productivity machine in too many cases. Everything can't be solved in a 30-minute meeting. We have to see leaders as people and they have to see us as people, and then we can share in a judgment-free zone. This requires maturation as a human being. We have to understand that the C-suite built the culture that suits the business, so rather than working to change it, we have to learn to influence it through our leaders."

In recent years I have become particularly passionate about equipping and supporting women in playing at the top of their game in business—and in life. As a coach, consultant, and human being, I have seen the energy that is unleashed through a simple shift in perspective. I submit to you that the cavalry isn't coming—it's already here, and it looks just like you! We invite you to add your voice as we continue along the journey of equipping women in corporations in getting the respect, recognition, and reward they have earned.

Olivet Jones

Olivet Jones is recognized as a premier consultant to Fortune 500 and global companies who want to have a more engaged, productive, and inclusive workforce and culture. Olivet consults as a strategic partner and certified executive coach to organizations, teams and individuals. She has been featured on ABC's *20/20* as a subject matter expert and was a former careers expert for Monster.com.

Under Olivet's leadership, her teams have worked on five continents in industries including engineering, finance, utilities, investments, brokerage, manufacturing, consumer goods, and more. Literally, her firm's work has taken her teams from the shop floor to the board room, always with an emphasis on tangible results.

In a recent interview, she stated: "We believe that engaged employees are mission critical in the current business environment. We work to identify and eliminate barriers to anything—systemic or interpersonal—that impedes that kind of culture. But I warn you: we don't do cookie-cutter. We'll draw from whatever discipline makes sense to help our clients get clear, get focused, and get into purposeful action. Our work isn't successful unless the client sees and experiences real change, real impact, and real results."

Today, her personal passion is the development of women and people of color to the highest levels of leadership. She is currently completing research on a field guide for corporate women that addresses "all the things I wish I had known 20 years ago!". Olivet invites you to share your story via email at:

jointheconversation@thecavalryisnotcoming.com

For more information on her diversity and inclusion work, please stop by www.felicitygroup.com or email her at connect@felicitygroup.com.

Whitney Martin

The Death of Guess:
Using Data to Make Better People-Related Decisions

Ever heard the expression "hope is not a strategy"? This phrase often pops into my mind when talking with HR practitioners about their hiring processes. Lurking beneath administratively burdensome screening systems that create an *appearance* of rigor, unstructured interviews, "gut feel," and other subjective criteria continue to weigh heavily in hiring decisions—we take our best *guess* and *hope* things will work out. However, while strong intuition and a good ability to "read" people are attributes that can prove beneficial in many contexts, they should not be the linch pin of employee selection, placement, promotion, or development decisions.

A profound change is occurring in the HR profession: business leaders are calling for HR to adopt a more evidence-based approach to decision-making. The frequency with which the terms *metrics*, *analytics*, and *big data* are creeping into HR circles is a testament to this. "We see CEOs and others wanting better data and not just a headcount report, but how is talent driving business results?" says Scott Pollak, a principal at PwC Saratoga in a *Harvard Business Review* report. With 57% of companies reporting their intention to have integrated, multi-source analytics in place in the next two years (according to another *Harvard Business Review* study), there is a push to incorporate more scientific, evidence-based practices in the people-functions in our businesses.

Based on some informal research, I've determined that exactly 98.64% of HR practitioners have, at best, a mild distaste for statistics. Therefore, there's an excellent chance that you may be experiencing some anxiety because of this demand for a more data-oriented approach to executing HR. Perhaps, too, this is why only 14% of businesses currently have data to show the business impact of their assessment strategy, according to an Aberdeen research study. So how do we infuse better data into key decisions throughout the employee lifecycle? And how do we measure the positive impact that HR is having on the metrics that matter most to the business? From hiring, through onboarding, coaching, career pathing, and leadership development, various assessment instruments can be incorporated to aid in decision-making, strategic planning, diagnosing root causes of performance issues, and developing solutions that work.

Hiring

With payroll and benefits representing one of the largest line items on virtually every company's operating statement, effective selection is one of the principal areas where HR can have a significant impact on the bottom line. But what kind of assessment instrument should you use in order to systematically select the best employees? The answer is a firm *it depends*. Follow the steps below to create a highly predictive, evidence-based, and quantifiably valuable selection system that works for your organization.

1. **Vision.** If companies had an unlimited budget (and candidates had endless time and patience) we could assess virtually anything—skills, knowledge, personality, values, attitudes, and the list goes on. But what are you *really* trying to accomplish? "We want to hire better people" is not nearly a clear enough goal. It is imperative to take the time, perhaps doing some research with internal stakeholders, to hone in on the ultimate goal for the company. Whether you're trying to impact retention, sales volume, early hire failure rate, patient satisfaction, customer retention, employee engagement, productivity, theft, absenteeism, safety incidents, scrap rates, or drug use in the workplace, there are different assessment instruments designed specifically to measure constructs that can directly impact these, and countless other, organizational issues or goals. Once your objective is clear, you can determine what you can measure that will help to predict that outcome specifically.

2. **Validity.** Take a moment and think about the best hiring decision you ever made. Jot down the steps in the process that moved that individual from a faceless applicant in the crowd to the super-star employee that exceeded all expectations. Now, think about the worst hiring decision you ever made—the "wolf in sheep's clothing" who turned disastrous. Did the hiring process that allowed the bad hire to get through the door differ from the one used when hiring the star? In all likelihood, the steps in both cases were nearly identical. After all, we develop our hiring processes with the goal of hiring the best employees every time—it's just that sometimes it works and sometimes it doesn't. Why? Simply because we're basing our hiring decisions on a combination of data points that lacks the ability to predict future job performance reliably.

Extensive research has been conducted on the *predictive validity*—the overall ability to predict job performance—of different hiring methods and measures, and some are just flat-out better predictors than others. Unfortunately, many practitioners continue to rely heavily on some of the least predictive measures, including interviews, reference checks, and four-quadrant personality assessments (not to mention "gut feel"). Well-developed assessments, including integrity tests, mental ability tests, and multi-measure tests (which incorporate a variety of constructs) can greatly increase your odds of making outstanding hiring decisions more often. The key is to find an instrument that measures the most appropriate combination of constructs to predict the well-defined outcomes you identified in the first (Vision) step.

3. **Verification.** Once you know what you're trying to accomplish (Vision) and the kinds of instruments that have a high degree of accuracy (Validity) in getting you there, you still need to choose an instrument from the hundreds (if not thousands) that are available in the marketplace. Considering the aforementioned fact that most HR people don't choose their profession due to their love of statistics, this part can be daunting. However, it's also necessary if you don't want to fall victim to the supreme sales skills of a vendor. If necessary, ask an Industrial-Organizational Psychologist from your local university to assist you in sifting through the technical validation documents provided by the vendor. Any tools used pre-hire must meet certain criteria as it relates to reliability, validity, adverse impact, and a number of other factors. Test publishers should be able to provide ample data showing how rigorous they were in developing their instruments.

4. **Value.** Now that you've developed a highly predictive selection process that is virtually guaranteed to move the needle on the metrics most essential to the business, it's time to quantify the impact that *your expertise* is having on the bottom line! You do this by demonstrating that the use of a particular tool is statistically correlated with what you're trying to predict. In other words, as test scores go up, turnover goes down, or as test scores go up, sales volume increases. Often, this can be achieved through either a concurrent or predictive validation study. Can you show a statistical correlation between how people score on the test you're using and how they perform on the job? If not, you may want to revisit the value you're getting from that tool.

It can't be stated strongly enough: your hiring process is destined for failure if the Vision step is not the bedrock for every decision subsequently made. As food for thought, let's contemplate an example we're all familiar with: pizza. Imagine your organization employs 20,000 pizza delivery drivers with an average annualized turnover of 170%. You know you can do a better job of "hiring better," but what specifically does that mean? Consider each of the following lines of thought:

A. As HR people, we understand the costs associated with turnover, so we begin to screen for factors such as reliability, work ethic, or other constructs that might enable us to hire longer-term employees. We'd measure our success by tracking reduction in turnover.

B. On second thought, since training for pizza delivery drivers is fairly minimal, perhaps turnover isn't actually that big of a deal. After all, all we really need are people who can zip to an address and hand someone a box, right? So let's screen for sense of urgency and sense of direction! We'd measure our success by tracking the rate of on-time deliveries.

C. But wait! Our drivers shouldn't zip *too* fast. After all, we need them to obey speed limits and demonstrate cautious driving practices. And, pizza delivery drivers handle a lot of cash, so we might also want to screen for integrity and safety. We'd measure our success by tracking cash discrepancies and driving incident rates.

D. And, gee, wouldn't it really differentiate our company (especially in the rather commoditized pizza market) if our drivers were also really friendly and engaging with customers? We could become the Southwest Airlines of the pizza biz! So, let's screen for friendly personalities and a passion for customer service. We'd measure our success by tracking customer satisfaction.

Each of the above is a completely valid and important strategy. Understanding which outcomes are going to have the *greatest impact* on the business will enable you to determine which combination of constructs is most important to measure.

Onboarding & Coaching
While you can gain substantial value from using assessments for employee selection, it's unfortunate when the benefits end there. By this point, the organization has made an investment, in both the tools and the candidate, and it should maximize that investment. Information gleaned from pre-hire assessments, or from other assessments

administered post-hire, can enable an organization to expedite onboarding and the identification of development needs by:

- Enabling managers to develop individually nuanced strategies for motivating, rewarding, and incentivizing new employees
- Facilitating a proactive dialogue between new hires and their manager on potential challenge areas and possible solutions
- Creating highly targeted employee development plans based on identified deficits in knowledge, skills, or behavioral tendencies

Armed with this knowledge, the new employee and their manager are set up for success, *proactively* addressing issues that could result in poor performance or lack of engagement.

Team Dynamics

While understanding the unique strengths, weaknesses, and tendencies of individual people is valuable, it's how those strengths are *leveraged* as part of a functional work group or team that really make an impact. Various assessment tools exist that allow you to look at the make-up of a group of people, including departments, special projects teams, leadership teams, and so on.

Imagine a group of leaders, for example. We might see that, while we have many on the team who are inspirational, creative, and energetic, we have few that excel at execution and managing details. Do we need to bring someone onto the team that excels in different areas to balance the team out? Do we need to engineer processes to make sure that no details fall through the cracks? Do we need to look to the individual on the team who is *most skilled* at handling detail work and ask him or her to play to that strength for the benefit of the group? All are valid strategies, and having good team data will enable you to make an informed and intentional strategic business decision.

Leadership Development & Career Pathing

Various types of assessment tools can play an invaluable role in supporting leadership development. Self-report assessments of personality, mental ability, passions and strengths, leadership style, or numerous other factors can provide insight into a leader's (or potential leader's) capacity and approach, and where development may be needed for peak performance, both now and in future roles. For example, training or coaching may be necessary to help a leader who is naturally conflict-avoidant to behave more effectively and confidently in situations that require them to be direct, firm, or confrontational.

Another tool that can provide essential data for a leader's development is 360-degree feedback. 360-degree feedback tools are designed to solicit feedback from critical "stakeholders" in the manager's success, including their boss, peers, direct reports, customers, board members, and so on. 360 data can provide essential information at both the "micro" and "macro" level. At the "micro," or individual level, the information from a 360 can form the basis of a highly targeted development strategy, then be used to measure the leader's developmental progress over time. If 360-degree feedback is gathered on multiple managers in the organization, the data can be aggregated and analyzed at a "macro" level to determine if certain developmental needs appear to be systemic in the organization, or whether leaders' strengths align with the organization's culture, priorities, and unique selling proposition.

For example, imagine your organization's success hinges on innovation. Suppose a macro-level analysis of 360 data reveals that 6 out of 8 of your top leaders struggle with "thinking creatively" (which is comprised of behaviors such as inspiring innovation, taking bold and calculated risks, and viewing obstacles as opportunities for creative change). This is a problem! Is the organization hiring leaders who lack the ability or propensity to think creatively? Does the organization's culture actually squelch out-of-the-box thinking despite claims to the contrary? Or, do we simply need to provide these leaders with more tools to enable them to innovate? In this case, 360 data has revealed a weakness that could literally mean life or death to the organization. And, additional assessment and survey tools can be used to provide more illuminating data for diagnosing the root cause of these issues so that an effective strategy to address this crippling deficit can be developed.

One Word of Caution

One size does not necessarily fit all (okay, more like seven words). The ultimate goal of a well-developed pre-hire assessment system is to predict future job performance. This may mean utilizing assessments that measure more stable, "hard-wired" characteristics that are not likely to change over time. So, how does that type of assessment lend itself to supporting training and development? Consider, as an example, someone who scores low on "assertiveness." It is not appropriate to think that training can turn this individual into an assertive person. Rather, training may allow the person to develop *adaptive* behaviors that allow them to demonstrate assertiveness when a situation calls for it. It is important to understand the nature of what the tool is measuring to ensure appropriate use of this information post-hire.

On the other hand, many assessments commonly used for post-hire applications— four-quadrant personality assessments, or communication- or leadership-style assessments, for example—are not ideal for use pre-hire. While there are many tools that lend themselves nicely to multiple applications, it's critical to make sure all parties understand the exact nature of the tool, what it's measuring, and the appropriate and inappropriate ways to internalize and apply the information gleaned from it.

The Death of Guess

Are you feeling pressure to incorporate more data-supported or evidence-based methods in your job? Is there anything you can do to increase the predictive validity of your hiring process? If pressed, could you tell your C-Suite exactly how accurate your selection system is and quantify the return on investment (ROI) for your efforts? Are you actually *leveraging* data gathered during the hiring process to inform post-hire activities?

The time has come for HR to embrace more data-driven, scientific methods for making key people decisions. Will you rise to the challenge? Well-placed and appropriately leveraged assessment instruments can be a relatively simple, cost-effective way for organizations of any size to infuse more objective data into people decisions—and to quantify the impact that the HR function makes on the metrics that matter most to the business.

Whitney Martin

As a measurement strategist, Whitney's passion and expertise lies in the field of surveys and assessments. A self-professed "data nerd," Whitney has a Master's Degree in the area of Human Resources Measurement and Evaluation and has conducted extensive research on the predictive validity of various hiring assessment strategies.

In 2003, Whitney formed ProActive Consulting, which specializes in delivering data-supported insights into job candidates, employees, teams, leaders, customers, and organizations through the integration of various assessment and survey tools.

Whitney has been a highly rated speaker at the National SHRM and SHRM Talent Management conferences. Both the *Harvard Business Review* and the Association for Talent Development have recruited her to write articles about assessments, and she has been quoted in *HR Magazine* as an expert on assessments. She is also a contributing author in the 2015 HR anthology *What's Next in Human Resources* (her chapter is entitled "Hiring Under the Microscope: Improving the Science of Selection") and the 2015 leadership anthology *HOPE for Leaders Unabridged* (her chapter is entitled "Creating an Evidence-Based Coaching Culture").

Whitney lives in Louisville, Kentucky with her husband and two young daughters. She is a member of the American Psychological Association (APA), the Society for Industrial & Organizational Psychology (SIOP), and the International Personnel Assessment Council (IPAC).

Whitney Martin, MS
336-202-2385
www.consultproactive.com

Robert Price

The Employment Ministry

My *Employment Ministry* began when I first heard these words: *helping people succeed!*

In December 1995, I was working as a sales manager for a Louisville company that abruptly sold. My separation phone call came at 5:30pm exactly six days before Christmas. When I hung up the phone, I was moved to devastation—but a simple peace came over me, and I was able to tell myself: it's going to be okay!

My wife, Renée, a homemaker, was with our three children at church, where they were leading a Christmas ministry project in support of children of inmates. If not for my wife and her many volunteers, those kids wouldn't have had a Christmas—but the church volunteers joyfully filled over 6,000 stockings that would soon be sent to jails and prisons in Kentucky and southern Indiana. The atmosphere was electric!

With the evening almost over, I took Renée aside and shared the news of my phone call. As I spoke, tears filled her eyes, but she seemed to have the same thought. "It's going to be okay," she said. Ministerial minds must think alike! We both knew God had bigger plans, and the peace we experienced must have been a manifestation of God's promise!

For I know the plans I have for you, declares the Lord, plans to prosper
you and not to harm you, plans to give you a hope and a future.
— Jeremiah 29:11

God led us to take a risk and open a small business. With nothing but hopes, dreams, and very little cash, we decided to open a food service brokerage business on April 1, 1996. Immediately, the blessings came pouring in; our business grew exponentially! Our business was doing so well in the years after it started that it caught the attention of a businessman who made us an offer we couldn't refuse (no, not that kind). One term of the sale was a one-year employment contract which gave me time and flexibility to evaluate my past and focus on God's plan for our future.

My wife and I visited a franchise broker in downtown Louisville. After taking some general aptitude tests, we were guided to the Express Employment Professionals franchise that we would wind up owning (and still own today).

I remember the words *helping people succeed*. These words penetrated our hearts and reached deep into our soul, and they have never let go! We were smitten with the Express vision: "*To help as many people as possible find good jobs, by helping as many companies as possible find good people!*"

This meant an opportunity for us to build a better life for our clients and associates. We had the courage to risk failure, but were guided by the values and principles we shared. The opportunity to purchase the Express franchise was very appealing to us indeed—"Where do we sign up?" we asked.

Through private business and church work, we learned how to lead and assimilate people in pursuit of a common goal. We knew there would be heartaches and disappointments along the way. Each time they came along, we kept faith in God's promises.

But there was still an untapped longing in my heart. I had a natural desire to pastor a "small church" of some kind; you might call it a *calling*. I wanted to help a congregation, however large or small, to fully realize God's plan, in the way I could see He was shaping my future.

Renée and I bought our first Express franchise in August 2006 and opened the doors of our Louisville office on November 6. We opened our second office in New Albany, Indiana on November 5, 2012.

While attending a new owner training class in Oklahoma City, I had the good fortune to spend a few moments with the Express founder and CEO, Bob Funk. I shared with Bob how I had sensed the call to ministry.

With a smile as big as Texas, Bob said, "Robert, you *are* in the ministry! We help people find employment that meets their families' needs, that puts a roof over their heads, clothes on their backs, food on their tables, and peace in their minds. You *are* in the ministry."

Both of our offices found immediate success by following the *Expressway* business model. Having a clear purpose and a values-based approach to business proved to be the right, and just, thing to do. It soon became apparent that more of the plan for our lives was being revealed to us: we found total delight in *helping people succeed!* Still, the real test of our resolve was yet to come.

Kalli Britton, an Express Developer from Florida, warned us "not to be discouraged when people break our hearts." She must have seen the ministerial glimmer in our eyes. Kalli knew our hopes and dreams could be dashed by employee disengagement, that it could risk client dissatisfaction or even failure in the long run. The thought of a *no call no show* never entered our minds. The thought of anyone having a work ethic other than mine never really crossed my mind. I thought, everyone else was raised just like me . . . weren't they?

The harsh reality is that people have individual hurts, habits, and hang-ups that sometimes hold them back from realizing their fullest potential.

Will my associates always perform their work at the highest level? Probably not, unless they're perfect or work for a truly perfect leader. For most people, most of the time, the answer is a flat *no*. As we know by now, people will quit a poor boss every time; people don't leave companies, they leave other people.

It became apparent to me that workforce training could be the *secret sauce* that could help set apart our business from the others. Our screening processes have always been second to none, but how do you instill dependability, good attitudes, and high levels of performance in the associate? My desire to succeed, as well as to minister to people, compelled me to become a teacher.

Everyone deserves a business hero; mine was Jack Smalley. Jack, an Express speaker and coach (and SPHR), traveled the country sharing employment best practices in a fun and exciting way. Whenever Jack spoke, I was riveted watching him command attention on subjects crucial to everyone's professional lives. Jack was giving sage advice and wisdom to a group of people *in need* of timely answers. I wanted to be like Jack.

I requested, and was granted permission to obtain, much of the Express PowerPoint material that Jack had used on the road. Evidently, my passion for HR, coupled with my own real-life stories and insights, had struck a nerve with attendees! I became known for my passionate delivery of an Express library full of leadership training classes.

Word spread like wildfire, and soon our staff began receiving training requests on a variety of subjects and challenges. Soon, requests were coming from clients and even companies we hadn't done business with. "Please help my managers learn how to *lead* their people!" some of them wrote to us.

As it turns out, people buy into the leader before they buy into the vision. Leadership is not about titles, positions, or org-charts; it's about one life influencing another. This requires a marathon-like commitment, not just the willingness to run an occasional hundred-yard dash. Managers must first buy in to the required marathon if they hope to be effective.

Entrepreneur magazine named Express Employment Professionals the number one staffing franchise in the U.S. for the fifth consecutive year! Express ranks seventieth in the magazine's Top 100 list of the top global franchises. This didn't happen by accident or coincidence!

I believe that culture is at the heart of any organization. Our values-based approach to *helping people succeed* is the reason Express is the second-largest privately-held staffing company in the U.S. with annual sales over three billion dollars.

Ronald Reagan once said, "The best social program is a job." A thriving economy dictates a job for every person and a person for every job. Reagan also said, "The greatest leader is not necessarily the one who does the greatest things. He is the one that gets people to do the greatest things."

Inspiring people to higher heights of service is at the core of good leadership. Good leaders know how to instill dignity, courage, self-worth, and a reason to believe in oneself (quite possibly for the first time).

Express has never been driven by the almighty Dollar; we are driven by Almighty God. We are champion dream-builders in a world of turmoil and strife; we are beacons of hope to our associates and the companies we represent. We have a higher purpose—

and, certainly speaking for myself, I have found a higher calling. That's why I offer my teaching time for free—you see, I am in the *Employment Ministry*!

Sound a bit cliché? I can assure you, it isn't in practice! The Employment Ministry is happening throughout the year . . .

- *Express Clothes Closet*—It's all about the fit! We ensure that our Office Services and Professional candidates "fit" our client's job profile. In many cases, they do not have professional-looking clothes that fit. Our Clothes Closet is open to any candidate that needs the blessing of a new work suit or pair of shoes!
- *Express Brand It Blue*—Every June, we celebrate our work anniversary by sponsoring a food collection drive with companies all over Louisville. We believe "Doing Good in Our Communities" a wonderful way to give back, so we partner with our local food bank, Dare to Care, to collect thousands of pounds of nonperishable food every year.
- *Express Pay It Forward*—Express provides a Thanksgiving meal to needy families during Thanksgiving and Christmas each year. To help make this happen, we partner with companies to put people to work, and a portion of the profitability goes to support this worthwhile ministry! (If you would like to nominate a family, please get in touch with the author.)
- *Express Children's Miracle Network partnership*—Express raises tens of thousands of dollars to benefit CMN hospitals. Any personal profits made from the sale of this book will be donated to Kosair Children's Hospital.
- *The Express Clydesdales*—Our corporate ambassadors of strength and courage travel North America to appear on behalf of almost 800 Express offices during special occasions. The Express Clydesdales have appeared in the Pegasus Parade during the Kentucky Derby Festival. Clients, employees and associates were invited to ride in a vintage 1880's stagecoach or walk alongside in parades.

It also happens in different forms of focused, needs-based training. *Monday Morning Leadership* is by far the most requested class that I offer! This four-hour course teaches managers *how* to become better leaders. We not only discuss, but *define* the differences between a manager and a leader.

I am continuously amazed at the number of former attendees that I sometimes meet in public. They greet me with, "Hello Mr. Price, I know the Main Thing!" or "My buckets are full of motivation!" With greetings like these, I am confident my classes are moving the needles of productivity and profitability in the right direction. I receive frequent requests for one-to-one coaching or one-hour refresher sessions.

Most managers are promoted from the production floor after demonstrating a better-than-average work ethic and good productivity. The rational conclusion by upper management carries the hope that, when promoted into management, their high-performance value will translate into an entire team of high performers.

The new manager leaves the impromptu promotion, celebrating their success. They've gotten a raise, but unfortunately, their short stroll down the hallway meets reality. Reality screams, "*Help! I've been promoted!*" No longer is showing up for work on time, or doing the job the way I've always done it, going to be good enough!

"Now that I'm a manager, the big boss expects me to actually *lead* people! How will I communicate, motivate and create a sustainable passion with the members of my team?"

Monday Morning Leadership includes eight mentoring sessions you can't afford to miss, namely:

1. Drivers and Passengers
2. Keeping the Main Thing the Main Thing
3. Escape from Management Land
4. The "Do Right" Rule
5. Hire Tough
6. Do Less or Work Faster
7. Buckets and Dippers
8. Entering the Learning Zone

These leadership insights will meet each person right where they live! The book and workbook are highly recommended at a cost of $10 per set plus shipping. We recommend giving each attendee at least two weeks of time to read the book. Trust me, once they start reading they won't be able to put it down! (Order and class information can be obtained by getting in touch with the author. Contact information can be found at the conclusion of this chapter.)

The ideal attendee is anyone within the business or organization that has people reporting to them. Additionally, you may want to give consideration to including your current Rising Stars!

Rising Stars are fun . . . Falling Stars are not! On many occasions, Falling Stars quit their boss and leave (hence, their designation as Falling Stars). Of course, the fault may lie with the poor manager. In my years of coaching people, I have seen, on numerous occasions, Super Stars at the pinnacle of success begin to fall backwards! Why?

The manager forgot about or avoided them! They willingly placed more work on the backs of their Rising Star performers and focused their energy on Falling Stars by allowing them to stay on the team without fear of consequence. The result? The Rising Stars quit after becoming Falling Stars of their own! I hear these tragic stories all the time.

There are so many candidates looking for work. When they find acceptable employment, they soon find themselves leaving a similar position as before, unable to cope. They either quit or get fired . . . and so it can go, over and over again!

We started a Second Chance class for associates who repeatedly met a similar fate. Some associates have low expectations in life or possess a low self-esteem or a poor work ethic! Our Second Chance classes are held in my office every Friday at 10AM. As an employment minister, I get to teach good work habits, dependability, and how to be a key contributor to the health, wealth, and vitality of the organization.

God has used my Second Chance class as a pulpit for me to share my faith in Christ with attendees. Why shouldn't I? God gave me a second chance! To my amazement, God opened this door; I just walked through and asked Him to speak through me! The result, to my humble joy, has been that people are turning their lives around.

Being an employment minister to my associates, employees, and clients is a job that I cherish. It's a ministry that I never thought I would find, but the minister in me is fed by giving back to my community and business family.

Below is a selection of Express classes I would be happy to teach to your teams. Each one is a ministry all by itself (and there are others)!

- Generations: The Five Faces of Change
- Make Time Work for You
- We're Hiring—Choose Well, Manage Well
- A Peacock in the Land of Penguins: Harnessing the Creativity of Differences
- First Impressions—Dress for Success!
- Effective Management of Turnover—Understanding the Costs
- Millennials: Do You Change Them, Ignore them, or Join Them?

My staff and I are richly blessed by the work we do. So, you see, I am not just the owner of a local staffing company; I am in the Employment Ministry.

May the Almighty continue to light your way during times of darkness; may he protect you and hold us together in our mutual Employment Ministries of service and helping people (and businesses) to succeed. It's the right and just thing to do!

Robert Price

EUCP

Robert Price celebrated 20 years in private business on April 1, 2016. His most significant accomplishment, however, is marrying his wife Renée thirty-five years ago, on May 16, 1981. Robert and Renée are proud parents of three; they are also grandparents of four beautiful grandchildren with another on the way!

Robert and Renée grew up in church and have always tried to follow the Golden Rule. Treat others the way you want others to treat you. Their dedication to the Lord and each other has never failed them!

It is with great pride and satisfaction that Robert has brought his chapter to you. Please do enjoy it!

Matthew 6:33

Owner, Express Employment Professionals
4919C Dixie Highway, Louisville KY 40216 (O: 502-449-6000)
3423 Grant Line Road, New Albany IN 47150 (O: 812-944-1600)

Robert.price@expresspros.com
www.expresspros.com
www.expresslouisvillejobs.com

Sandy Ringer

The Elusive Butterfly:
HR's Role in the Evolution of Coaching

The future of coaching seems nebulous to some—but if it were truly embraced by HR, it would strengthen every person working for an organization, and in turn it would strengthen the organization. Why is there confusion surrounding coaching? Here's a test—what do the following have in common?

- Leadership transition
- Questioning a career
- Team alignment
- Attitude and behavior disruptions
- Family business dynamics

You guessed it—all can be coached! As you can imagine, in many of those cases it's difficult, elusive, and downright uncomfortable coaching!

So, first, let's be clear. I'm not talking about those critical conversations that should happen often with associates. Hopefully we have the nerve, willpower, and desire to communicate in those situations. Hey, that's coaching too, but in a different internal way. It's tough enough to keep up with this type of coaching, yet alone add to the fray; however, HR must get more comfortable with critical conversations.

I know HR is extremely busy with compliance, new laws, benefits, and keeping the organization out of trouble. For HR, outsourced coaching may not be at the top of their minds. HR may wonder about the cost-to-value ratio and may fear (or wrongfully assume) that it will be too costly for its benefits. Coaching enables leaders to develop in ways that no other modality can.

So let's talk about some real life coaching situations to demonstrate benefit and value.

Coaching Scenario #1

We were introduced through an attorney and a company incident. We stayed together because the coachee was hungry to learn, eager to change, and wanted to think and process differently – and increase his own awareness. The company contributed to six months of coaching because he was an extremely valuable individual to the operation. He invested in himself for another six months. He had this to say:

> "You have to want to be coached and be ready for it. If not, it doesn't work. Coaching helped me better understand me – my strengths, opportunities, and how to interpret it without a blow to my ego. It was firm but fair, open and caring, and always profession-al. I was very at ease with the process. It defined a different protocol in how I learn, how I relate to people and to the business. It continues to be a building block that bene-fits me long-term in my career. I've learned to be more focused in my learning process, setting priorities and being disciplined—focusing on direction. I have a higher regard for people, which is what leadership is all about."

All this from the Vice President of a large national retailer—he put it well, so I'll add nothing else.

Coaching Scenario #2

Their challenges: new team members, stress-inducing and demanding bosses, health concerns, and a need for new coping skills to improve not only work but overall life balance. The coachee wanted to learn new ways of being a creative leader while holding others accountable and empowering the team. Planning and executing were paramount in this position (in this case, the Vice President within a large healthcare system!).

> "My professional development was tremendously enhanced by the engagement with an executive coach. I was grateful to have the opportunity to interview for the best match and without reservation I instantaneously knew she was the best fit. She was interested, engaged, insightful, and clearly had a wealth of knowledge in compliment-ing my experience and rounding out my weaknesses. We are so dedicated to our roles and responsibilities that it can be difficult to take the time to stop, reflect, and listen to a mentor with a different perspective. My coach helped me shore up my weaknesses and develop a well-rounded skill set for the stage in my professional development. Her insight in guiding me in my decisions was one of the most effective learning experienc-es of my professional career."

Coaching Scenario #3

In this case: two managers in the same location had a critical need to work together in operations, but they could not get along with one another—hence, it began to erode the entire team within that facility. The managers appeared passive-aggressive, would undermine one another, and would compel divisive behaviors. Their leader was baffled by all of the behaviors and attitudes, so coaching was offered to each manager.

Six months later, one manager career-transitioned out of the organization. The second manager remained in coaching and rebuilt a solid team that became stronger because clear goals were established and the team was empowered to make good decisions. Operations within that facility grew. The coachee began to coach team members so everyone benefitted from the coaching experience. (These were two managers from a mid-size division within a large utility organization.)

Coaching Scenario #4

An autocratic team leader leading a group of eight to ten fabricators discovered the power of listening and "not needing to have all the answers." Over a relatively short coaching period, he was raving about new ideas in production, new ways of working, and good suggestions brought forth by his team members. He was amazed and thought he had uncovered the key to leadership. He had come a long way in changing his own behavior toward his team.

The result: through his coaching process, the team leader attributed new attitudes and behaviors to developing a more trusting team, willing to talk with one another, and offered ideas that really worked in their environment. Continuous improvement at its best. (He was a team line leader in a mid-sized manufacturing company.)

So what's the process, the secret ingredient to coaching? *Getting to the heart.* It's about the relationship and trust. It's creating an environment of openness, acceptance, and non-judging for the coachee. When these factors align, then it's about allowing the process to unfold.

To me, each individual I coach is like a blank page—only I don't do the writing, the participant does. It is that person's time to focus and find the answers from within. As a coach, I might assist in clearing up definitions or offering probing questions for heightened self-discovery, but they do all the internalized work. My job is to get to the inner core, whatever that might be—to get to the heart of the matter. That's where people change and have those *aha* moments. That's when coaching starts to work! This may sound unusual, but the solution to the coachee's issues lies within themselves. After all, people are much more likely to engage with solutions that they have discovered themselves rather than those that are forced upon them.

Coaching does three things. First, it focuses on the future. Second, it fosters performance within a business context and often migrates to purpose, balance, and becoming a better leader. Third, it assists coachees in discovering their own inner self and path, their true values, and how they want to be perceived before leaving this world. This is all extremely positive for the employer, HR, and the coachee.

I believe that unleashing the full power of an organization starts with unleashing the full power of a single person. Coaching significantly improves personal and professional skill sets and enables people to find more balance, think more critically, feel more in control, feel empowered, and remain capable of giving the greatest possible contribution to the organization. When an organization's people move into a zone of optimum sustainable best performance, so does the organization. And, to the fortune of many, offering impactful executive coaching engagements for a wide range of leaders has never been easier.

The reasons for seeking coaching are linked to a desire for change at one or more of the following levels:

- *Intrapersonal*, or how to be more effective unto yourself;
- *Interpersonal*, or the desire to develop productive relationships; and
- *Organizational*, or developing leadership and promotional change.

A coachee's ability to positively change behavior at any one of these levels brings significant benefit to the entire organization. There is a growing opportunity for HR to make a strategic impact on leader development, change management, succession planning, and more through executive coaching.

What Should HR Look For in a Coach?

- Good chemistry between the coach and coachee—have the coachee interview the coach.
- A solid methodology—what, for example, does "discovery" look like? Is there a 360 feedback? Are there interviews to gain discovery? Does the coach use different assessment tools?
- Who is in the know? Is it outlined ahead of time? How will confidentiality be managed?
- What do the "touch points" look and sound like?
- Is there a contract between the coachee and coach and a clear understanding of the process, with areas of accountability?
- Can the coach achieve results? What has been the coach's past performance? Are there references?
- What does the engagement look like for all the parties? Is there a general plan or timetable?
- Internally, who will provide insight and feedback to the coach regarding the coaching experience?
- What are the potential outcomes for the coaching event?

Evolution of Coaching in Business

You don't need to reinvent a model. The majority of companies will utilize coaches for leadership transitions, where either the leader has been promoted or is getting ready to be promoted, and the organization wants to invest in key critical skills for the individual to increase their success. Today, organizations are moving toward developing and implementing a 'coaching system' where one call will serve to start the process. The focus is on developing high-potential leaders. Many times I've heard, "I don't really know what to do next" or "I'm not sure how to get through all these tough organizational changes."

Even when organizations know that executive coaching could bring tremendous benefit, most don't have the time, resources, or expertise to design and manage a strategic coaching program independently. One of the best ways these organizations can maximize the return on their coaching investment, without a long learning curve or significant internal resource demands, is to engage a reputable executive coaching firm. The firm must have capabilities to design and manage coaching programs that are closely aligned to organization objectives and executed by highly qualified coaches. I often part-ner with Point C Business Consultancy, which offers cost-effective executive coaching to organizations whether they are looking to support one leader or one hundred. Their methodology makes executive coaching turnkey with a proven coaching model, lead-er-driven coach selection, consistent measurement of results, and one point of contact for program management. Programs like these make it easy for organizations of any size to tap into the power and promise of executive coaching.

Determining the ROI of Coaching

How do you measure the value of leadership, and even more, the value of developing leadership to accelerate the executives' future impact within the organization? A study of a global survey by PriceWaterhouseCoopers and the Association Resource Centre in January 2012 found that the mean return on investment in coaching was seven times the initial investment. Over a quarter of coaching clients reported stunning ROIs rank-ing from 10 to 49 times the cost of coaching.

Coaching is an organizational investment. How do you measure in dollars the impact of leadership development—learning new skills, enhancing critical skills and experience, performing at a higher level within the organization and with other associates, and improving overall personal effectiveness? How do you place a dollar figure on being a better husband or wife, father or mother, community member, and every other aspect of one's life, since leadership coaching impacts the individual's total person?

The Evolution is Happening

Coaching does not need to be nebulous or elusive. The process of coaching addresses learning, reactions, behaviors, and results.

Envision a time in the future when your company has an evolved coaching model and process for developing leadership, for assisting in delivering desired change: in the way we communicate, the way we spend time, the way we acquire new behaviors and skills, the way we create high-performance teams, or other key factors that define the leadership and direction of the future. With one call, HR can become more resourceful while saving time and delivering a creative solution for enhancing leaders within the organization. I have learned that whatever the reason and whatever the value, coaching can make a huge difference with individuals, and ultimately with the organization as a whole. So how can coaching be leveraged in the future?

- HR needs to keep coaching top-of-mind.
- HR can leverage best practices.
- Be affirmative and positive. Coaching yields positive outcomes.
- Engaging outside coaches offers an easy support system.
- Coaching provides strong organizational support – "We want our executives to be successful!"
- Coaching ensures that outsiders and consultants understand the organization's culture and goals.
- Coaching fosters a useful understanding of how each leader is unique and will have unique needs for development and support.

If you have an opportunity to enhance operations by sharing some of the workload with professional coaches, why not? The end outcome is improved results, and both the numbers and the people validate that. The need for executive coaching in organizations is growing rapidly—so the time is now, and there are easy ways to make it successful.

Sandy Ringer
PHR, SHRM-CP

Sandy Ringer is currently President and CEO of Business Visions in Louisville, KY. As a business strategist, coach, and Human Resources professional for more than 25 years, Sandy's strengths include business planning, executive/managerial/team coaching, leadership and family business transitions, and HR consulting.

Sandy's real value comes from honest communications, asking the right questions, and developing relationships of trust and strong processes. Because of this, she has helped increase sales, produce team alignment, create new business opportunities, and develop internal systems to improve management and assist revenue growth. She has facilitated visioning processes with CEOs and coached management teams for improved alignment. Her "partnership" with her clients offers a unique advantage to them.

Sandy's experience in consulting includes a broad array of industries—manufacturing, professional services, construction, healthcare, and nonprofits.

Sandy gained national recognition serving as a United States representative to the USSR under the auspices of The American Center for International Leadership.

Sandy is active within her own community—a graduate of Leadership Louisville, a facilitator of several CEO Roundtables, a Board member with New Hope Service, a Board Advisor for the Business School at Spalding University, and a career mentor. Sandy is a member of the Society for Human Resources Management (SHRM) and the local Louisville chapter (LSHRM).

Contact Sandy by email at <u>Sandy@bizvisionsconsulting.com</u>, 502-718-7749, or at <u>linkedin.com/in/sandyringer</u>

Cassandra Tembo

Performance, from Monitoring to Managing to Maximizing

In any work environment, employee performance is a key indicator of the organization's overall effectiveness. The organization will not be successful in achieving its mission and vision if the individuals making up the organization are not performing at the right level. Moreover, individual success—one person performing well—doesn't at all mean the team or organization is succeeding. Often, the collective strength of an effective team is greater than the sum of their individual strengths; conversely, the collective strength of an ineffective team may be less than the sum of their individual strengths, especially when the team isn't unified by clear common goals. As with performance and talent maximization, it isn't always about good versus poor performers; sometimes it's more about effective fit for the role. We often refer to the right person in the right seat, but we must go further—to consider the right leadership style with the right rewards and recognition, the right culture, and so on and so forth. It is not simply a matter of intelligence and dedication.

Over time, Human Resources professionals and management teams have evolved their view of the leader's role and purpose in affecting employee performance. At first, their (our) approach might have been more tactical, and perhaps quantitative in tracking the employee's performance against a checklist of deliverables. (Picture a quality control associate with a clipboard, standing over the person's shoulder monitoring and documenting performance notes.)

As we moved from just charting and checking, we began to see the real value of this information: to identify deficiencies, address them, and drive improved performance through talent development and workable action plans. This approach was more effective than the incessant performance documenting; still, with little support beyond a routine performance evaluation, managing performance in this way placed excessive focus on weaknesses and often left the person hearing criticism of what they weren't doing, rather than praise for what they were doing. There was an attempt to soften the blows by referring to weaknesses as "development opportunities," but in the end the person was still left focusing on a seemingly insurmountable list of personal improvements. Performance management felt like pushing someone from behind—perhaps too fast or too slow or in the wrong direction altogether. Performance maximization, on the other hand, moves us from the monitoring approach of checklists and ratings to focus on actually developing talent, with action plans that focus not only on performance gaps, but on leveraging the individual's strengths and creating team dynamics that truly exceed individual capabilities. As one of my favorite managers used to say, two heads are better than one.

Performance maximization is beyond individual effort and ability. It is building teams encompassing the right mix of strengths, with a strategy to leverage those strengths to achieve results with, through, and for the individuals making up the team.

In an election year, it's easy to apply the principles of performance monitoring, management, and maximization when observing how the candidates communicate. Some focus primarily on the checklist; they discuss what they have accomplished in the past while highlighting what their opponents have not accomplished. They sometimes do this without clear context for that past performance and how it may translate to future performance. Others spend time ensuring voters recognize certain "performance weaknesses" in their opponents without providing the balanced view of their opponents' strengths. Politicians, in other words, speak in terms of performance monitoring and management; what they often critically miss, or what politics in general is missing, is a drive to leverage the right combination of strengths in a political system (or party) that would generate the best outcomes, even if that means steps like crossing party lines to drive the best candidates into political leadership. As within many businesses, it doesn't (always) happen that way, and in politics at least, many people feel they are left only to elect the "lesser of the evils," that they are forced to accept the gaps in their candidate's knowledge, skills, or experience.

Key Components to Maximize Performance

When we think of employee performance, we think about clearly defined goals, effective performance assessments, and development plans to manage performance. Performance maximization goes beyond these fundamentals to include what I call RAFI:

Relationships that are mutually beneficial and built on trust
Agility in leadership style and approach to processes
Feedback that is ongoing, actionable, and inclusive of strengths and positives
Investment on the part of both the employee and the organization

Perhaps the most critical aspect in helping individuals achieve their greatest potential is the relationship with their leader. Engagement surveys and research continue to indicate: employees stay in (or leave) an organization mostly because of their direct supervisor. When it comes to performance maximization, trust is a key driver at every stage. The pace of business often leaves the impression that there isn't time to foster meaningful relationships in the workplace, but the payback is always worth the time invested.

The need for trust is even more critical when we consider the growing quandary of generational diversity in the workplace. The self-motivated Traditionalist and Baby Boomer generations saw work as a necessity and accepted the established reward; they simply came to work and did their job. Millennials, on the other hand, need to know their contributions matter and require frequent positive reinforcement. They look for upward mobility as a sign of value.

Beyond generational differences, we continue to understand more about personality preferences through instruments like Myers-Briggs, DiSC®, and Predictive Index®. Thus, it is incumbent upon the leader to connect with team members individually and adjust their own approach to create an environment that allows each person to thrive.

In one manufacturing environment, the plant manager required his direct reports to know personal facts about the employees (to the extent employees were open to share them). The plant manager would walk up to his direct reports and ask a question about a production worker's family. While it was initially uncomfortable and felt insincere to some, engaging in personal dialogue eventually became a delightful habit that allowed managers to express value in individuals beyond their work contribution. Needless to say, employees became more inclined to exert discretionary effort in support of the manager who appeared to care about them and their family. It was as simple as scheduling time each week to walk the production floor and pause for brief informal conversations; some management even learned to take their breaks on the production floor instead of in the break room. It does require a commitment of time and energy to ensure that the urgent demands of the day don't supersede the important relationship-building that fosters trust and personal dignity at work.

One of the key benefits of these improved relationships is a mutual trust that facilitates honest feedback from the leader, accompanied by the employee's open receptivity. Employees are naturally more responsive to both positive and constructive feedback when they believe their leader genuinely cares. This caring aspect, combined with leadership agility, will result in feedback presented in the best manner possible for the individual. Effective feedback is actionable feedback; effective feedback leaves someone knowing what to start, stop, or continue doing. Notice that it is just as vital to know what to continue doing as it is to understand what to stop doing. Positive feedback is often more powerful than constructive feedback; this aspect of performance maximization focuses on leveraging strengths rather than highlighting weaknesses that, in some cases, may not even be worth the effort to address.

In one experience, a young professional had not responded effectively to his manager's feedback. As we began to develop a performance improvement plan, we realized he was likely to fail due to self-imposed stress if we presented him with the standard template for improvement plans. We decided to alter the approach, and instead of giving him the typical document stating he was on a 90-day improvement plan, we implemented all components of that plan without presenting the standardized document to him. As with typical improvement plans, his manager met with him regularly to review expectations and provide her assessment of his performance against the goals presented. The meetings emphasized where he excelled and how he could demonstrate the same skills in other aspects of his role. This painted a very different picture from what employees often imagine of performance improvement plans—that they are concentrated efforts to document their (deficient) performance in preparation for involuntary termination. Likewise, at the interim assessment meetings, we generated the standard documentation but did not present any documents to him. It was clear the increased meeting frequency and detailed expectations he was receiving generated what we'd hoped for him: a stated intention and motivation to perform better. Changing our approach not only salvaged a potential talent, but boosted him; he was rated in the top 10% of employees the following year.

This example also demonstrates the value of seeing talent as an investment on the part of both the organization and the individual. Too often, employees are labeled as poor performers and the focus becomes shooing them out in hopes of finding a superior replacement. The time, cost, training, and development should all be viewed as investments. What company *doesn't* want to generate significant return on investment from the money they spend? What company, then, would ignore investing in their human capital?

The person invests in the organization, too. Therefore, they deserve an opportunity to understand how they can reach their greatest potential by taking responsibility for their contribution and receiving the right support from their managers and co-workers. One manager I worked with commonly asked: First, do they know what to do? Second, are they capable of doing it? Third, do they want to do it? This became my litmus test for whether or not further investment was worthwhile for the organization or the individual. If they aren't capable or don't want to perform, the best support may be to help them find a role better suited for their skills and experience.

Second Corinthians 12:9 tells us His strength is made perfect in our weakness. Part of the collective strength of a team that leads to maximizing performance is recognizing other individuals' strengths and, in turn, being able to admit your own weaknesses. Performance maximization is about taking the best and making it better, not "fitting a square peg into a round hole".

Once you apply the RAFI approach to performance maximization, remember to work hard, play hard, and celebrate hard. We all deserve it!

Cassandra Tembo

Cassandra Tembo is the Vice President of Administration for Cedar Lake, a non-profit organization that supports adults with intellectual and developmental disabilities. In this capacity she is responsible for both the Human Resources and Finance functions.

Cassandra's professional mantra is "achieving business results with, through, and for people" because she believes employees show up every day with a desire to contribute their best to achieve exceptional outcomes. Results are not just for customers and stakeholders.

Cassandra graduated *summa cum laude* from North Carolina Central University with an Accounting degree and earned a Masters in Industrial and Labor Relations from Cornell University. She maintained a Certified Public Accountant license for eighteen years while progressing from Deloitte and Touche's audit function to Plant Controller/Logistics Leader at Corning, Incorporated. After graduate school, she joined PPG Industries, Inc. where she was US Employment and Compensation Manager for the Architectural Coatings business, Americas Human Resources Manager, and then Global Human Resources Director for the Packaging Coatings business.

Cassandra has served on boards and advisory committees for Big Brothers/Big Sisters of New River Valley and Hospice of Raleigh. She has been a member of the National Association of Black Accountants, Society for Human Resources Management, and American Society for Healthcare Human Resources Administration. Cassandra is passionate about the opportunity to make a difference in marketplace ministry. She has shared the love of Christ across the US, as well as mission trips to Zambia and Novosibirsk. She resides in Louisville, Kentucky with her husband Kedrick.

Trasee Whitaker

Innovation-Inspired Human Resources

Prior to joining the Masonic Homes of Kentucky in 2010, I gained work experience in retail, non-profit service organization, and legal services. Each different business implemented innovation in different ways, and in each case I had the opportunity to be involved in some way. At the same time, I was a volunteer leader for the Society for Human Resource Management (SHRM) and was influencing change at the local, state, and national levels. My experience as a human resources professional, combined with the volunteer leadership roles, gave me exposure to culture change and innovation. I felt prepared to move into a role in healthcare. Little did I know that I was about to embark on the journey of a lifetime, that I would become completely immersed in a world of innovation, that I would develop a strong passion for our business and for the people we serve.

Ultimately this is the story of how Human Resources is influenced, challenged, and inspired by the constant flow of innovation at the Masonic Homes of Kentucky. To set the stage, I want to share the MHKY story and the visionary leadership that set the stage for this incredible journey.

What is Innovation? A new idea, device, or method.

The moon landing was watched in 1969 with awe by millions huddled around black-and-white television sets with their families and friends. Fast forward to 2016 and we are Tweeting with astronaut Scott Kelly through a daily Twitter feed he uses during his year-long journey in space. His tweets featured magnificent photos of the universe, planets, and the occasional selfie. Imagine what the world would be like if innovation for space exploration stopped when we landed on the moon, or if screens and consumer technology stopped developing only when color television reached half of American households. Hard though this alternate universe is to imagine, we might have been stuck with TV and radio as the end-all and be-all for news and electronic media; the only exploration of the universe might have been through novels and comic books.

Great innovators push through failure and criticism to stay true to their vision, passion, and belief that a better product or service will greatly benefit and revolutionize society. Steve Jobs purchased Pixar and expected it to make money, of all things, as the next great hardware company—yet he had the courage to support the Pixar founders' dream to produce a full-length, digitally-animated film that would transform the entertainment industry. *Toy Story* was released and the rest is history.

A marketing innovation that drew both criticism and cheers—and increased out-of-state student enrollment—when the University of Oregon donned fluorescent sports uniforms, creating a nationwide buzz (and some significant new merchandising opportunities). Oregon recently unveiled plans for the world's first LED football field to keep the brand fresh and fluorescent.

Innovation abounds in all businesses, regardless of industry or profession. Masonic Homes sets the standard for innovation in senior living.

Masonic Homes of Kentucky—Passionate People. Inspiring Lives.
Founded in 1867, the Masonic Homes of Kentucky has an extensive history of providing quality care to older adults and children. The demand for senior living services increases significantly every day and will not slow down anytime soon. Baby Boomers expect the ultimate successful aging experience, along with an impressive menu of amenities and care options. Masonic Homes embraces the opportunity to develop and offer innovative services that differentiate us from other providers.

Everything that we do must support our purpose statement—*passionate people inspiring lives*—and line up with at least one core value.

Our core values, in no order, are:
- Innovation
- Growth
- Passion
- Remarkable Service

We have implemented, piloted or modified more than 30 technology and 100 operational innovations since 2011. (2007 is when we began thinking innovatively, when we began saying *what if we did this?*)

Significant growth began when The Sam Swope Care Center opened on our Louisville campus in 2011 and set the standard for short-stay recovery and long-term care communities by deinstitutionalizing the traditional nursing home model (the spatial orientation in each household is similar in setup to the design of a typical family home). We have opened many new business lines and expansions since then.

Sproutlings Pediatric Day Care & Preschool provides spaces for both medically fragile and typical children, which in turn allow every child to learn, play, and grow with one another. Sproutlings is the only integrated model that we know of in Kentucky.

The Miralea Active Lifestyle Community offers an unparalleled lifestyle with an extraordinary array of amenities and services to meet the needs of adults who are at least 62 years of age, and is the only community in Kentucky to offer life care, providing estate protection and health care assurance. Two years after its opening, Miralea underwent an expansion that would add 30 apartments and underground parking facilities.

The Village Active Lifestyle Community business model was reinvented to include a life plan component and additional amenities. FirstLight HomeCare at Masonic Homes now offers companion care and personal care. In addition, two businesses are currently under construction and scheduled to open in 2018: Grove Point Assisted Living and The Meadow Active Lifestyle Community. Strategic growth opportunities for the next five years include identifying opportunities for new services, expanding business on our Shelbyville campus, and providing new services and community outreach on the Louisville campus.

Innovative Leadership, Expectations, and Results

"There is a way to do it better—find it." This quote is formally attributed to Thomas Edison, but it could just as easily have been coined by Gary Marsh.

Gary Marsh, President & CEO of Masonic Homes of Kentucky, inspires our leadership team to embrace innovation and bring new ideas to the table; he is always pushing us to find a better way to do it. He has more than 40 years of experience meeting the needs of the senior population; thus, Gary is a natural mentor and role model to every-one on our senior leadership team. Gary has often said that his vision for MHKY has been enhanced by the strength of our team because we are all equally passionate about our residents, employees, and a real desire to be the premier service provider with what we do for people.

Gary describes his experience with innovation this way:

> "For many years I have had an interest in the advancement of innovation and technol-ogy and often experiencing more frustration than success. I recognized early on in my career that meeting the needs of our senior population would require constant change. In the last five years, there has been an explosion of new innovation and technology to serve the senior population. With the creation of the "Thrive Alliance," made up of forward-thinking non-profit senior living providers from around the country, and the new "Thrive Innovation Center" in Louisville, Kentucky, we are pioneering the future by influencing the creation of high-quality products and services that meet the needs of our rapidly-growing senior population. It just so happens I am one of those people."

We've encountered many stops and starts with innovation, especially in technology. Let me give you a head start: expect failure and frustration. Approach failure with the right attitude; treat it as a blessing and not a curse. Dust yourself off and keep dreaming big.

Some of our innovations include:
- Multiple accounting and clinical systems modified to meet our changing needs;
- WiFi silent non-visual nurse call system,
- Electronic medicine locking systems with real-time data,
- Interactive staff communication and resident alert system,
- iPod responders and tablet communication devices,
- Smart watches for memory-care residents,
- Monitoring systems,
- Electronic move-in and admission processes,
- Automation of many human resources processes—and more.

MHKY is recognized as the leader in the senior living industry. Gary Marsh and J. Scott Judy (our COO) have presented the MHKY innovation story at more than 10 national, regional, and state conferences, plus to CEO round-tables. Fifteen senior living leaders have been on our campus to experience our innovative best practices firsthand to consider for adoption in their own communities.

Human Resources Innovation

Implementing, piloting, and modifying 30 technology and 100 operational innovations company-wide created opportunities and challenges for me personally and for human resource initiatives at MHKY. First, I had to rethink what innovation means to me and what it means to the practice of HR. I had to commit and consciously focus on supporting the culture of innovation. At the same time, I had to find solutions to remove the labor-intensive transactional work to free up more time for our employees to focus on the real work: the delivery of remarkable service and care.

Six HR processes have been automated; two are headed that way. Many programs have been developed and launched: customized remarkable service training, above-and-beyond recognition and rewards programs linked to our core values, stay interviews, wellness program designed by our employees. A HRIS was implemented with the new financial software. Our IT department developed an employee status change portal and database. Next up is a performance management and compensation dashboard to link performance to rewards; a new orientation program will also roll out this month, including segments that can be pushed out prior to the employee's first day.

All of these initiatives include significant development and support from our talented IT and communications teams, plus leadership at all levels. Our corporate HR team includes me, a HR coordinator, an administrative assistant, and a part time generalist; the four of us serve more than 650 employees.

Innovation Chats

In late 2015, the corporate HR team started hosting quarterly innovation chats. Their purpose is to keep innovation fresh and to look at problem-solving through different lenses with collaboration and input from throughout the organization.

A core group of influential leaders, line managers, and staff share their big ideas and new information, then identify the roadblocks to employee engagement and brainstorm solutions for them. Guest speakers are invited to speak on topics of interest; already this has proven to be invaluable. This creative group developed three innovative initiatives in the first two chat events.

Prepare to Switch Gears: Think "Innovative," Not "Transactional and Compliance"

Leave your ego at the door. You may be the content expert, but that doesn't necessarily make you the solution expert. Build trusting relationships with your team members and ask for their opinions and ideas; be prepared to hear the good and bad, and learn how to not take it personally.

Leave your office. Invest time and energy in building a network of collaborative people who are doing great things for their industry or profession.

John Reinhart, co-founder of Thrive Alliance, brings senior care providers together with cutting edge technology and service vendors to explore innovation and opportunities for synergy. John gives this advice:

> "Today's environment, especially in healthcare, has created the necessity for organizations to align with a multitude of partners. In many circumstances, the parties that would benefit significantly from full cooperation may not fully understand each other's perspectives. Developing the innovative approach of "coopetition" has emerged as a key differentiator for organizations. *The key challenge for talent management leaders is how to instill a partnering mindset to their stakeholders and at the same time protect their 'secret sauce.'"* (Emphasis added.)

Leave regulatory compliance out of brainstorming sessions. There is always a way to build in compliance after the big idea takes shape—you're not breaking any rules just by brainstorming! For example, electronic employee background checks was one of the first HR processes that we automated. The regulatory auditors were unfamiliar with this format and we had to educate them on how the data would be collected and how we would remain compliant. The changes did go through, and without any compliance issues; it goes to show that innovation can thrive regardless of, and sometimes in spite of, compliance issues.

Jumpstart Innovation

"You miss 100% of the shots you don't take."
— *Wayne Gretzky*

The development and implementation of a line manager training program has been a source of frustration. We tried several solutions and nothing would stick. The innovative chat team came up with a concept and we now are working on the 'how.'

To get to the solution, we followed these steps:

1—Ask Why, What If, and How*

Why. Ask why five times (more or less). *Why is it not working? Why don't they like it? Why are we struggling with attendance? Why is it difficult to implement? Why do performance issues go unaddressed?*

What If. Ask what-if questions to spark imaginative thinking. *What if we offered sessions online? What does our clinical learning solution offer? What if we ask their preferences? What if we start a book club? What if we don't do anything?*

How. Use how questions to focus on how to implement the 'what-if' ideas. *How would it work? How can we make it convenient? How can we find the materials? How can we follow up on the results of learning? How can we make it fun?*

*As outlined by Warren Berger in A More Beautiful Question: The Power of Inquiry to Spark Breakthrough Ideas (Bloomsbury Publishing, 2014).

2—Write Objectives

For example: A manager is participating in training which will be delivered via mobile learning in a bite-sized learning format. We want to know who participates, how they used the learning, and how this impacted employee retention.

Tell prospective vendors your desired outcome(s), then restate them in a follow-up email or phone call before their presentation or demo. The sales person will usually be the first point of contact and needs to clearly understand your objectives. We love to preview fresh innovation, but sometimes it isn't fully developed or the sales person may not fully understand how it works yet! Adrian Judy (our CIO) and I previewed a very cool learning platform recently; more than once the vendor answered our questions with "We will have to think about that" or "No one has asked us that question before." We ask stronger questions, anticipate pitfalls, and refer to our previous mistakes when previewing innovative products—that way we avoid being blinded by that shiny, new solution.

3—Implementation

The fun of innovation usually ends just before the next most important step: implementation. We have learned through trial and error these essential details:

- *Project Timeline*—Spell it out step by step.
- *Budget*—Expect the unexpected. Know the numbers.
- *Contract*—Read every line, have legal counsel review it, and understand what terminating the contract early could mean.
- *Training*—Who will be trained? When and where? Who will prepare for and conduct the training? What resources will you need to conduct the initial training?
- *Communication*—Make sure that you have involved key stakeholders in the process before the new program is announced. Their input, as well as the input of the people on the front lines, is invaluable in the entire process.
- *Replacement*—If it's a replacement system, will data need to be migrated to the new system? Who will perform the migration? Will systems need to be run concurrently for a time, and if so, how long?
- *Equipment*—What equipment or materials are needed? Does this need to be purchased or can you rent it if it's not necessary to keep it past training?

The evolution of human resources is a work in progress at the Masonic Homes of Kentucky. Innovation for innovation's sake is not the goal. Nor is ROI the most important thing to us; the most important thing is that we create a better living environment for our residents and create more opportunities for our amazing and passionate employees to do what they do best: to give remarkable service and care to the residents and children that we serve.

Trasee Whitaker

SPHR, SHRM-SCP

Trasee Whitaker is the Senior Vice President of Human Resources and Chief Human Resource Officer for the Masonic Homes of Kentucky, Inc. Trasee leads all aspects of human resources and develops initiatives that support Masonic Homes' business strategy and core values: remarkable service, passion, growth and innovation. She has more than 25 years of human resource experience in a variety of industries and professions including legal services, a nonprofit service organization, and retail management.

Trasee currently serves as a regional representative on the Advocacy Committee for the American Society for Healthcare Human Resources Administration (ASHHRA). She previously served as Chair of the Kentucky Society for Human Resource Management (KY SHRM) and President of the Louisville Society for Human Resource Management (LSHRM).

Trasee received her Bachelor of Arts degree in Communications from the Ohio State University and holds the designations of Senior Professional in Human Resources (SPHR) and SHRM Senior Certified Professional (SHRM-SCP). She enjoys boating and cheering for the Buckeyes.

Trasee can be reached at twhitaker@mhky.com. You can also visit the Masonic Homes website at www.masonichomesky.com, and you may reach Trasee at (502)445-1544.

Patricia Keene Williams

Why Did I Get Married?
HR's Role in Sustaining Employer-Employee Relationships

Why did I get married? Why do *most people* get married? Love, if that's the reason, is the most powerful emotion that any human being can experience. It's the powerful newness of a relationship, the excitement of the unknown—love is attractive, sexy, endearing. But a wise person once said: "Falling in love is easy. Staying there . . . therein lies the challenge." I couldn't agree more!

I am sure that you're asking how love and marriage relate to this phenomenon we call *the evolution of Human Resources*. It's simple: people are changing. This means that the human resource function in organizations must change as well. I make the argument here that the longevity of employer-employee relationships are just as emotionally motivated as the longevity of a marriage. So, how can Human Resources professionals help keep both employers *and* employees engaged and committed? It is the evidence of two-way communication, trust, shared vision and collaborative growth that most create loyalty in these relationships; this is the recipe for a flourishing employer-employee relationship that will stand the test of time. Here's why and how.

When pondering the question *why did I get married?*, it is important to also think about why you might get divorced. What are your personal non-negotiables? What would have to take place for you to judge the relationship issues irreconcilable? These are critical topics that should be discussed after hiring a new employee. Think of it as pre-marriage counseling: once you've made this commitment, it is imperative to know what it will take from both parties to sustain the relationship.

I have often heard our present time referred to as the "microwave era." The idea is that this is a period in time when people crave efficiency, bore easily, and (most) tend to prefer quality over quantity. The demands of technology and innovation are ever-present! Almost everything is done fast. Everyone is busy and thinking towards tomorrow. Employees want to move up the ranks more quickly than ever before. The implication is that the United States is, more and more, on the move! Millennials (Americans born between 1981 and 2000) are increasingly entering the workforce with expectations that are totally different from their Generation X (1965-1980) and Baby Boomer (1946-1964) predecessors. Scott Berridge concludes, through his research, that Millennials have a far less committed attitude about marriage, property, and life because of their experience of the Great Recession of 2008 (Berridge, 2014).

Does this mean that Millennials are incapable of loyalty? I don't think so; they just need something they can trust. As Boomers continue to retire and the presence of Millennials in the workforce grows stronger, human resources has to place an intentional focus on creating loyalty within the employment relationship.

Remember how exciting it was to start a new job *or* a new relationship? The butterflies that invaded your stomach as you pushed through the interview and selection processes (or first dates) were all worth it. Anyone would be naturally delighted to be selected for a position and surviving and conquering the extensive HR processes between the person and that union. The eagerness to learn everything about the company and the position is often overwhelming. Most employees accept a job with the drive to perform well—but employees soon lose that drive if there are not deliberate efforts being made to groom the relationship they now have with their employer. The relationship is the nucleus, the basis for whether the employee chooses to work hard at the same company for one year, five years, or ten years—or not at all. The goal of Human Resources should be to retain the warmth of the honeymoon phase; this happens through a continuous process of learning from each other and providing the individual support that is required.

Communication is key! There is absolute value in communication simply because people want to be included. Do not be so closed to innovative styles of communication as well; less seasoned workers may prefer a text or an email over a phone conversation. Appeal to that sense of comfort, but also recognize that this is where they are comfortable because this is *their* culture. I have found myself laughing on several occasions at one of my teenagers for texting me a question while we sit in the same house, only a few rooms apart on the same hallway. In their own time, Millennials have not been trained to communicate verbally for their primary method of communication, given their seemingly-unlimited access to technology and its non-verbal means; therefore, employers have to cultivate those abilities in them if they are necessary for progression in that company or work environment.

How do you keep employees engaged? Employees want to be part of conversations about changes in the organization that affect them, and they want their opinions and feedback to be seriously considered before major decisions are made. A wife who continuously makes decisions about finances or the children without consulting with her husband is, more than likely, going to experience some marital problems. In the long run, communication is non-negotiable! Communication is the ingredient that keeps the employer-employee relationship healthy and remembering why they "fell in love." If I'm remembering why I fell in love, I'm remembering the reasons I got married, and therefore my opportunity (and desire) to become distracted by "competitors" is much smaller.

Lies are relationship-killers. Once a lie is uncovered, it's almost impossible to recover the trust that was present beforehand. So be honest! Management and Human Resources teams must be open and straightforward with employees about everything from expectations to career progression path. Today's workforce must be positioned for growth and opportunity; they won't hang around if they feel misled or stuck.

According to a 2014 Allstate National Journal Heartland Monitor Poll, 60 percent of Millennial workers leave employers within three years. Human Resources has a responsibility to improve this turnover. We do this by purposefully keeping the vows to love, honor and cherish the relationship. Do what you say you will!

The ambition of the workforce in 2016 for upward movement is, unarguably, stronger than it has ever been. We are all dealing with a more educated workforce than we had before, which means, among other things, that there is considerably more student debt among incoming workers than at any point in our history. Some believe that Millennials want high dollars that they have not yet earned; whether this is true or not, it's not hard to understand why they want to get the most bucks for their bang.

So, for one important point, Human Resources professionals have to consider the benefit of formal education and begin teaching *application* of those skills and knowledge in real-world situations. As more and more Millennials pervade the workforce over the next three to five years, there will be less talent available with heavy work experience. Therefore, the more innovative businesses will create on-the-job training and development plans that will teach soft skills, decision-making, and leadership.

For another point, I believe Millennials *can* be loyal. I recommend full transparency and a detailed development path that is realistic and achievable. If employees are engaged, they are generally better stabilized.

One of the cavities frequently discussed in human resources-related conversations is the divide between employers and employees about the vision of the organization at the high and low levels, including the foreseeable future of that particular employee. This should not be kept secret. Collaborative coversations need to happen on a recurring basis to assess performance and determine what the company is working towards. A person doesn't know what they don't know. If your spouse hates sleeping with the television on but she never tells you, you wouldn't know to turn it off, would you? We can't limit our conversations simply to annual performance reviews, to the matters we all know we have to discuss. If we do that, that's when employees "divorce" before the next annual review comes around. Again: feedback, goalsetting, and development must be a continuous plan that is reviewed and updated at regular intervals.

Why is this a topic of interest? Nationally, there is high-level dialogue taking place about the skills and talent gaps across the United States and the forecasts that these disparities are going to worsen over the next five years as the workforce continues to transition. There is a clear shortage of talent in the skills needed for performance in certain industries.

What is the action that the human resource body can take? *This* is it. In our innovative thinking process, is there training or education that the employer can supply to create the talent needed internally? Be sensitive to the individual needs of your employees. Succession planning needs to happen sooner. Start making training and development investments in high potential talent early. This is a joint retention and succession effort. Why did I get married? What does it take for a Millennial worker to invest ten years in a single organization? They don't stay for mere gratitude of having a job; employees, like spouses, still want and need to grow in their own ways.

I have given you broad responses to this question at the Human Resources level. It is still vitally important that conversations happen that meet individual employee needs. Remember, "staying in love" isn't easy. Human Resources is a conduit to facilitate communication between management and the employee that will remind them both why they "got married." Employees fall in love with organizations that communicate, keep promises, practice inclusion, and intentionally work to develop them. Does your organization practice these things? If the answer is no, it is definitely the time to schedule a strategic planning session. Divorce is costly!

It's no secret that employee turnover causes real damage. A successful Human Resources function and management team are defined by the performance and professional development of their teams. There has to be a more calculated concentration on these relationships—so let's learn how to stay married!

Further Reading
- Berridge, S. (2014). Millennials after the great recession. *Bureau of Labor Statistics: Monthly*
- *Labor Review*. Retrieved from United States Department of Labor database (2014).
- Attention, employers: Millennials have made their demands. *The Atlantic*.

Patricia Keene Williams

CSP, MSM, MCSM

Patricia Keene Williams is a passionate Human Resources Professional and an advocate for workforce development. She is a Ph.D. candidate at Sullivan University Systems, where she plans to use her research as a platform to introduce strategies for developing employability skills in a changing organizational climate. Patricia holds dual Masters Degrees: one in Conflict Management, another in Management. She also holds a Bachelor of Science Degree in Human Resources Leadership.

Professionally, Patricia works for LG&E KU Energy in Louisville, KY as a Human Resources Associate. She also serves as Director of Workforce Readiness for Louisville Society of Human Resources Management (LSHRM) where she leads development initiatives aimed to improve workforce skills and strengthen talent pools. She has been recognized by LSHRM for her relentless volunteer contributions and also received a Kentucky Colonel Award from Governor Steve Beshear in 2014 in honor of her service to the community.

When Patricia is not working, she enjoys being a mom to her children Austin, Alarria, and Aiden.

Patricia believes that giving back is not an option, but a shared responsibility that is given to each individual. One of her favorite quotes is from Og Mandino: "Always do your best. What you plant now, you will harvest later."

To contact Patricia for human resource consulting, please email her at patriciakeenewilliams@gmail.com.

Lisa Withers

Proof Positive:
The Case for Positive Feedback

Mark Twain once said, "I can live for two months on a good compliment." For me, it's been more like two decades now.

When I was in college, I had one of those professors that most students try to avoid. She had a reputation for being hard; in reality, she had very high and precise standards. When she returned our first paper of the semester, mine was sprinkled with red, indicating my frequent grammatical and formatting errors—but at the top was a message that said, "Good work. Your writing demonstrates an exceptional command of the concepts through your use of examples."

This wasn't the first time I had made a good grade, but this *was* the first time I recall getting specific, positive feedback beyond the obligatory "good job." It caused me to think that my skill and contribution could be unique and valuable. At the time, I was struggling to figure out what I wanted to be when I grew up; that comment changed the trajectory of my career and my life. I shifted my focus from broadcasting to organizational development; I went on to graduate school to study under that same professor. To date, I have logged over 20 years in training and development, 13 as an independent consultant. I am proof positive of the power of positive feedback.

The Bottom Line on Feedback

At work, positive feedback often gets laughed off as one of those "soft" topics for serious business people . However, positive feedback can produce some of the most serious business results.

Research has consistently demonstrated a strong return on investment for employees feeling appreciated and valued. The benefits include increased daily attendance, decreased tardiness, closer compliance with policies and procedures, reduced conflict among staff, increased productivity, and higher customer satisfaction.

Most organizations measure their overall organizational success through some combination of profitability, productivity, customer satisfaction, and employee retention.

When it comes to employee retention, positive feedback has its most obvious impact. If you've made the case for intentional retention efforts, know that positive feedback is a means to that end. If you create a workplace where people feel valued and appreciated, they are more likely to stay—period. In fact, the US Department of Labor reports that 65% of people leave their jobs because they didn't feel valued or appreciated, making it the number one reason for turnover in the United States. Gallup's research indicates that employees who feel they are not adequately recognized at work are three times more likely to say they will leave the following year.

Let's look at those "harder" numbers. Consider Gallup's Q12, the 12 questions that, according to Gallup, best predict work group performance. Teams that scored in the top quartile on the Q12 are 56% more likely to have higher-than-average customer satisfaction scores, 38% more likely to have above-average productivity, and 27% are more likely to report higher profitability.

One question in particular is responsible for a 10 to 20 percent difference in revenue and productivity. That question is: *In the last seven days, have you been praised or recognized for doing good work?* I don't know of an organization who wouldn't want 10 to 20 percent gains in revenue or productivity; those are serious business results! At the same time, I don't see many organizations clamoring at this opportunity they can take simply by making better use of positive feedback. Instead, in my experience, I find it much more likely that organizations invest in costlier solutions that don't produce the same results.

For example: in their quest to be the best place to work, many organizations make considerable investments in training and rewards programs to drive satisfaction and engagement scores. That kind of investment is a testimony to the tremendous job HR professionals have done in elevating engagement and the value of corporate culture. I applaud that commitment and believe it vital to organizational effectiveness—*but*, unfortunately, positive feedback is often simply overlooked in the overall strategy. Instead we opt for—as I said—more costly and less impactful solutions.

Evidence suggests that, every day, informal recognition has far more employee impact than formal recognition programs. The Recognition Management Institute reports that frequent recognition practices are three times more impactful on employee engagement than formal recognition programs.

Have you ever noticed that there is never **Breaking *Good* News?** If your regularly scheduled TV show is overtaken by a news desk, it is never for good news. There are no tests of the "good news broadcasting system," *beep beep beep.* It's as if good news just isn't worthy of stopping what we're doing; only bad news can come suddenly. Many of our organizational effectiveness strategies reveal the same bias in favor of "constructive" feedback—which most often means constructive criticism. For the purposes of this chapter and for contrast, "constructive" feedback refers to feedback that points to deficiencies and needed improvements, as opposed to positive feedback, which aims to highlight and acknowledge strengths and accomplishments. We don't bother to provide the positive parts because, most of the time, they just don't seem urgent in the same way "constructive" feedback might.

Our feedback-gathering mechanisms are often predisposed to finding the opportunities for improvement, and therefore, by default, de-emphasizing the positive. Unlike our countless methods for finding and fixing problems, we simply don't favor systems for finding or focusing on what is working.

Focusing on the positive isn't new. While Ken Blanchard added it to our lexicon a quarter century ago with his book *Catch People Doing Something Right*, the field nowadays remains saturated with the sort of "constructive" feedback that doesn't align with the spirit and value of his work.

Feedback has long been recognized as an essential leadership skill. It is a staple in leadership development programs and a crucial element in performance management. However, the mantel for feedback is exclusively reserved for giving constructive feedback; positive feedback receives an honorable mention at best. It does not garner significant time or attention in leadership development or performance management.

In my 20 years of designing and delivering leadership programs, giving feedback is one of the most-requested training topics. The training request is almost singularly for constructive feedback: *teach leaders to effectively tell their employees when they are not meeting expectations.* And I will, as long as I can also teach them about the power of *positive* feedback. I want leaders to know that it is their *praise*, not their "constructive" feedback (no matter how well-delivered) that has the greatest potential to fuel performance. The American Psychology Association reports that employees who feel appreciated by their employers are 60% more likely to say they feel motivated to put forth their very best at work.

Again, this is not a case against constructive feedback unto itself. I am not suggesting we shift our training from constructive to purely positive. I believe it truly is critical that leaders know how to deliver constructive feedback effectively, since poorly-delivered constructive feedback can do considerable damage to performance and a working relationship. The consequences of messing up positive feedback, though, are not nearly as fatal; not giving positive feedback often enough (or at all) can be fatal, however. So while we should teach constructive feedback, we also need to evolve the appreciation for positive feedback by showing its impact on the bottom line.

At the end of my feedback training sessions with leaders, I issue a challenge. I ask the participants to think of their most challenging employee, and over the next week, to "catch them doing something right" and provide positive feedback to them. I ask leaders to email me with the outcome. While I can't give you data points here, I can tell you the emails often begin with *I was so surprised*—most often, the leader reports an unexpected behavior change, either in attitude or action.

Many leaders believe positive feedback is "nice to have," but little else. While most leaders acknowledge positive feedback can inflate employee satisfaction and engagement scores, their appreciation for appreciation ends there. Many leaders simply do not recognize positive feedback as anything more than mere acknowledgement of good performance.

A gratitude survey by the Templeton Foundation revealed that people are less likely to express gratitude at work than any place else in their lives. While I think we need to create a compelling case for leaders, I do not recommend a "program" per se to mandate the frequency of positive feedback—that, for example, leaders be required to write five thank-you notes per week. While doing thank-you notes would be one great way to demonstrate positive feedback, a mandate would rob you of the benefits. Leaders have to find ways to do it in sincere, earnest, context-sensitive ways.

You're the Best I've Ever Seen

There isn't a litany of best practices on how to give positive feedback (unlike the litany available for its fraternal twin, constructive feedback). I will offer two suggestions.

First, the feedback should be *specific*. Years ago, I interviewed for a training job. After my audition, something trainers know very well as part of the interview process, the very enthusiastic and positive hiring manager exclaimed to me, "You're the best I've ever seen!" That felt really good at the time. But after getting the job, I came to realize he had a team full of the "best he's ever seen," and I met another one of them every week, it seemed. It was a common platitude. Positive feedback is more powerful when it is specific and unique to a particular person.

Second, and the most important thing about positive feedback: *it must be sincere*. You cannot simply manufacture compliments and praise, or it won't serve its purpose. Once, at a gathering of extended family, there came one of those awkward silences when the dinner table conversation hit a lull. My well-intentioned brother-in-law broke the silence by complimenting the pinto beans made by my husband's grandmother— and for years after, there was not a gathering of that family without pinto beans and an extra-large bowl just for my brother in law. Years later, we learned that he never really liked pinto beans; he'd just been making polite conversation . Again, positive feedback is a powerful driver of performance; just make sure you are driving the right action with your sincere praise!

As you take your seat at the table, as HR professionals, you are constantly looking for innovative and impactful ways to drive performance and make measurable contributions to your organizations. You are committed to being good stewards of your organization's time, effort, and money. As you further evolve the role of HR, I implore you not to overlook the case for positive feedback.

Bestselling author Marcus Buckingham said it best: "Praise isn't merely a reaction to great performance. It is the cause of it."

Lisa Withers

Lisa Withers has over 20 years of experience leading training and development efforts for organizations. She is known for her witty and laugh-out-loud approach to topics like communication, feedback, and change.

Lisa takes abstract theories and models and turns them into practical tools and strategies for her audiences. She often draws on common life experiences, including her own as a wife and mother, for stories to demonstrate content in a relatable way. Lisa delivers the perfect combination of humor, energy, and usable content.

Lisa earned her B.A and M.A in Communication from UNC Greensboro. She not only turned her liberal arts degrees into a successful career, but a thriving business as well. She began her career providing in-house corporate training for targeted employee populations such as sales, customer service, operations, and leadership functions. Since 2003, Lisa has been at the helm of her own business, providing customized training programs to an impressive list of clients across the U.S.

For small organizations, Lisa often functions as the sole training and development professional by designing and implementing entire leadership development programs. For large organizations, Lisa is often a featured consultant complementing existing curriculums with her customized content and engaging delivery.

Lisa's programs are not prepackaged. Everything is "made to order." Lisa's in-depth comprehension of the nuances of corporate culture bolsters a keen ability to assess needs and implement successful learning customized for your organization. Lisa's business acumen, dynamic personality, and genuine approach to speaking and training helps her clients achieve real results. She makes measurable contributions to the companies with which she partners by identifying their unique needs and delivering effective learning that supports their distinct organizational objectives.

Lisa can be reached at www.consultproactive.com (see "Training & Coaching" under the Services tab) or on Facebook at "Lisa Withers Consultant."

CALLING ALL AUTHORS

Want to contribute to a *Professional Series* anthology? The *Professional Series* will continue in Fall 2016 with *Cultivating Culture*. We will begin accepting commitments on July 15, 2016; our publishing program will begin in September, and books will be published and available for print and sale in November.

Want to suggest a new anthology? Obviously, there are plenty of subjects we haven't covered yet. Whether you're a reader or a writer, we'd love to hear about the anthology you have in mind, so we welcome your suggestions for anthologies, whether for the *Professional Series* or a different series entirely. Of course, if you want to work on your own *title*, not just your own chapter . . .

We offer custom anthology services. If you're a subject-matter expert wanting to publish a focused anthology on your subject with your colleagues, or if you're an organization seeking to crystallize culture and open new marketing opportunities, a custom anthology might be right for you. Get in touch to discuss details.

How to Get Involved

- **Visit our website at** RedLetterPublishing.com/Anthologies to sign up (when available), ask any questions, propose topic suggestions, or inquire about custom projects. On our website, you can also find FAQs and information about previous anthologies and other publishing projects.

- **Contact us directly** by phone or email. To reach Kevin, you may call him at (502) 639-7789 or email him at Kevin@RedLetterPublishing.com. To reach Cathy, call her at (502) 445-6539 or email her at Cathy@CathyFyock.com.

CPSIA information can be obtained
at www.ICGtesting.com
Printed in the USA
LVOW12s0233130516

488063LV00001B/1/P